penduka

21 WAYS TO AWAKEN PASSION & PURPOSE IN EVERYDAY LIFE

Leah +

Blessings on your journey to awaken your soul!

+ Joy

JOY MCMILLAN

Scriptures taken from the Holy Bible, New International Version®,
NIV®. Copyright © 1973, 1978, 1984, 2011 by Biblica, Inc.™
Used by permission of Zondervan. All rights reserved worldwide.
www.zondervan.com The "NIV" and "New International Version"
are trademarks registered in the United States Patent
and Trademark Office by Biblica, Inc.™

ISBN-13: 978-0692567883
ISBN-10: 0692567887

DEDICATION

This book is dedicated to the amazing young women I've had the honor of mentoring and coaching, and to the many wise women who have poured their time, love and counsel into me over the past 20 years.

And to my mother who has not only sacrificed greatly to see my sisters and me bloom, but has modeled so beautifully the transformative power of unconditional love and relentless hope. You have taught us that an open heart and an open home were quite possibly the only way to live and love well. Sitting at your feet all these years has shaped and molded me into the woman I am today and I will be forever grateful.

CONTENTS

PROCESS

169

FINAL THOUGHTS

241

PREFACE

Welcome!

I believe with every fiber of my being that you were created for a purpose. That the breath in your lungs this very moment is a tangible reminder that you are alive today for a reason. I am thoroughly convinced that nothing about you is accidental.

The things that make your spirit dance.

Those things that make your soul ache.

And those things that come so naturally to you that you don't even consider them gifts. They are all breadcrumbs along the journey to discovering who you are and why you're here.

With that being said, I believe we over-think and therefore complicate the process.

We ache to live lives that matter, to do work that actually makes an impact on the world around us, and to weave a legacy of love and grace in the way we flesh out our days on this planet. We have an unmistakable sense of being a part of something greater, maybe even an inkling of what the part is that we play in the grand scheme, but so often we feel stuck. Ineffective. Unqualified. Unnoticed.

We wonder whether we'll ever actually get our act together.

We fear we'll be found out. That other's might see us the way we see ourselves; as a fraud or an impostor.

We look at what others are creating with their lives and wonder what's wrong with us.

Or we just feel too small and ordinary to really accomplish anything substantial or extraordinary with our lives.

We long for the extraordinary. Because we were created

for it. But we dismiss the ordinary in our never-ending search for the extra.

The good news is you're exactly *who* you're meant to be. And it's highly likely you're exactly *where* you're meant to be for this season.

So what if I told you that you - right where you are, with all those quirks and inadequacies, and yes, even those struggles and failures - have everything you need to succeed in this life already woven into the fabric of who you are. It's true, friend. It's all there. Tucked away down deep, like a seed nestled in tight. Full of potential and right on schedule.

We will unpack what it means to be consistent and faithful in the everyday. To show up, even when we don't feel like it, and to believe that in just being present and engaged, things are happening. Together we're going to unwrap some of the neatly packaged lies we've bought into that have kept us shackled, we'll press into and through the fear that holds us back, and we'll step into the life we've been created for.

INTRODUCTION

You're here, thumbing through these pages, because you're meant to be. It is no accident or coincidence that you were drawn to this book and that here you stand, ready to embark on a journey to wake up your soul.

If you purchased this book, you most likely have a fire in your belly. An ache to understand your unique purpose more fully, to live your life with more passion, and to use your time more effectively and with more intention.

If someone bought this book for you, they see that fire in you and want to call it to the surface.

How ever you ended up here, welcome. I'm excited to walk alongside you as we explore passion and purpose, along with another component that acts as the third leg of the Penduka stool, process. We'll pick up each concept, flip it over, unwrap and dissect it, and get a better handle on how each impact our lives on a day-to-day basis.

WHAT DOES IT MEAN

The word 'penduka' is distinctly Namibian. In the Oshiwambo and Otjiherero languages, spoken widely in this breath-taking country where I grew up, it means, "wake up!".

This book is a call to rise up and to step into who you were created to be. Not just in the big, flashy moments of life, but in the everyday. For it is out of the everyday that our stories are carved and our imprint made.

Penduka is a whisper of more and a battle cry of hope.

It is an opportunity to stop sleepwalking through life, to say *no* to numbly surviving and *yes* to a life lived fully alive.

This book is an open invitation to wake up your soul.

HOW TO READ THIS BOOK

When I initially set out to write Penduka it was a 3-week experience; 21 consecutive days of digging into these power-packed themes of passion and purpose and the process that actually puts skin in the game. I wanted us to fully immerse ourselves in the concepts and get our hands good and dirty.

But as I started to map out the skeleton, I realized that while this 'fire hydrant' style of consumption motivates some, it completely overwhelms others. You may prefer to take a sip from the fountain every few days, allowing what you imbibe to slowly soak in and assimilate. Getting blasted in the face isn't everyone's idea of a good time.

If you're a driven, goal-oriented gal, you may choose to set aside 21 days to work through it; fixed, focused and on a mission.

But if that isn't your preferred method of consumption - and if you're a strict rule-follower - consider this your permission to digest this at a pace that works for you. Maybe a chapter a week is more your style.

If you're more of a meanderer than a sprinter, you might find yourself picking through the table of contents and reading the chapter that resonates with you that day, returning for another nibble a week later. While this is okay, the concepts do build on each other and have intentionally been laid out in the order they are, so will have the greatest impact when worked through in order.

How ever you choose to read, I would urge you to read only one chapter a day. While it may be tempting to plow through this little book quickly, don't rush it. Allow it to soak in, challenge and encourage you, and empower you to take action.

Want to dig deeper?
Interested in hosting a small book study group?

The **Penduka Study Guide & Journal** is loaded with thought-provoking questions, journal prompts and action points for each chapter, making it a wonderful supplemental guide to the #pendukalife journey.

WHAT TO EXPECT

Each chapter is short enough to read in one sitting and is intended to give you something to chew on for the rest of the day. You'll find **Penduka Points** to ponder in each chapter, along with some of my favorite quotes peppered throughout.

The 21 chapters are divided up into 3 sections, each with a seven letter theme word and acronym:

PASSION | PURPOSE | PROCESS

In a nutshell; passion is the fuel, purpose is the direction, and process is the way in which we get there.

My goal over these next twenty-one chapters is not to quench your thirst. It's to make you thirstier. This won't be a one stop how-to shop that will satisfy your ache to live a life that matters in 21 easy steps. That would be selling you short.

I pray rather that it ignites something so deep inside you that every new day becomes a fresh opportunity to step more fully into who you were created to be, with stronger conviction and greater clarity.

It is my intention to ruin your appetite for the status quo, so yet another day lived on cruise control loses its appeal entirely.

I hope to help you engage with your purpose in a way that you'll wholeheartedly follow the breadcrumbs of passion, scattered throughout your life, so you can fully experience this one, wild and beautiful life with everything you've got.

While these 21 nuggets are simple, they won't always be easy. Knowledge is one thing, the discipline and determination to actually do something with what you know is another thing entirely. We all know we should eat less and move more, but actually implementing these principles into our lives is a whole 'nother ballgame. Head knowledge will not change your life any more than reading an exercise book will develop your core muscles. It requires action. Small and decisive, it's the thousands of little choices we make every single day that create a life of passion and purpose. And this is where the process comes in.

Accomplishing anything truly meaningful involves risk. Sometimes the risk is simply showing up again and again to do the work when it seems no one cares to notice it, and when it feels like your soul is starving for recognition. And then showing up again the next day.

Other times it's bringing your work out into the open,

allowing yourself to be seen, and risking rejection.

Maybe this time it's just mustering the courage to try again after exquisite failure.

Be willing to engage with risk, embrace your fear, and get your hands dirty. Our time here on earth is limited. We need to choose to live fully each day, for it is all we have.

In stepping up to the canvas day after day and applying a simple brush-stroke to the artwork of our lives, we will see a masterpiece - a legacy - beginning to take shape in the small, everyday moments of our lives.

God breathed something into you before the foundation of the earth, sweet friend, and it's your job to exhale it. There will never again, on the face of this planet, be another human being quite like you.

Welcome to the invitation of a life-time.

"Your visions will become clear
only when you can look
into your own heart.
Who looks outside, dreams;
who looks inside, awakes"

C.G. JUNG

"Every great dream
begins with a dreamer.
Always remember,
you have within you
the strength, the
patience, and the
passion to reach
for the stars to
change the world."

HARRIET TUBMAN

PASSION

"I would rather die of passion
than of boredom"

VINCENT VAN GOGH

What do you think of when you hear the word "passion"?
Young lovers? Raw energy?
Mother Teresa? The yummiest hibiscus-infused crimson
colored Tazo tea?
Enthusiastic support of a compelling cause?

You wouldn't be wrong if you listed any of the above. Passion
inspires and fuels many projects and people, but there's more
to it than that.

We are all guilty of cheapening words like passion and
love by declaring our passion for 'The Big Bang Theory' and

our love for pizza, followed by our declaration of passion for ending human trafficking and our love for our spouse. We forfeit the depth of what passion is when we dilute it with such broad brush strokes.

The word passion originates from the Latin word "passio", which has its root in the Greek word "pathos", meaning "suffering". Think: the Passion of The Christ. Despite the flowery sentiments often attached to the word, it is not synonymous with bliss and euphoria. It isn't just energy or fierce excitement. Passion feeds off and inspires these things, but it is compelled by something far deeper.

Bona fide passion has its eye on an end goal. It casts vision and demands focus, and fully acknowledges the process. It recognizes that there are risks and sacrifices involved but stands on the fact that temporary pain has an ultimate purpose.

The majority of society today runs on caffeine and adrenaline, with the occasional spike in enthusiasm. But mere enthusiasm won't get us far when obstacles block our view and troubles arise.

Happiness fizzles when the going gets tough, while passion pushes through.

Interest wanes when the journey seems boring, but passion is more invested. It has skin in the game, after all.

Excitement heads for the door when things get uncomfortable. Passion knows what's at stake and runs head-on towards the goal.

Passion is wholeheartedly committed to the end result.

We quickly find out what motivates us when what lies ahead gets uncomfortable, or the next big thing woos our attention away.

I've become excited over many things in my life. Scrapbooking. Teaching step aerobics. Boys with motorcycles. Designing baby announcements. Becoming a circus performer. All of these things peaked and then fizzled out as real life happened, I lost interest, or something better popped up on the horizon. I've started many things I haven't finished, not because they weren't good things, but because the momentary discomfort of fleshing them out revealed my lack of genuine commitment. I jumped ship the moment the water got choppy.

When we're not afraid to try something new, we learn quickly what we do enjoy, and what we don't. What we are passionate about, and what was just a phase. Or hormones.

I've experienced the temporary high of launching a new project or program, only to have the adrenaline wear off and think..."what on earth have I done? I don't want to do this!". And I've tasted the rush of success in something that makes me wonder, "maybe I was born for this?", only to realize it wasn't THE thing, it was merely a step toward THE thing.

While I'm not advocating becoming a quitter who doesn't follow through on commitments, rest assured it's normal and healthy to dabble in different things that excite our hearts. Assuming they're not illegal, destructive or dishonoring of others, these little adventures are all a part of the bigger picture and reveal aspects of ourselves we may not have identified before.

They act as breadcrumbs along the path to discovering what it is we truly are passionate about. They point to our passion.

The first step we're taking in waking up our souls, and the first stage of the Penduka triad, is passion. Let's unpack some of the key ingredients in tapping into it and stirring it up.

"When your passion & purpose are greater than your fears and excuses, you will find a way"
Nishan Panwar

CHAPTER 1

P | PURSUE JOY

"The gloom of the world is but
a shadow. Behind it, yet within
our reach, is joy. There is
radiance and glory in the
darkness, could we but see;
and to see we have only to look".

GIOVANNI GOCONDO

We could spend our lives chasing happiness, only to find it eludes us. While we know the fulfillment and bliss we seek doesn't come prepackaged as possessions, job titles or accomplishments, we still fall for the marketing. Those big, shiny things that are guaranteed to bring unending pleasure and contentment. More money. Less weight. Fuller hair. Bigger house. New man. In five easy steps and just three easy payments of $19.99, or your money back.

Far too much of my adolescent energy was spent chasing cute boys, a smaller waistline, or popularity. Not necessarily in that order and most likely all at the same time. Age landmarks beckoned from the distance too, promising all the perks and possibility of the next category of cool. When I was 12, I desperately wanted to be 16, but when that arrived, 18 was where it was at. And then 21. I spent the first 25 years dismissing the purpose and value of the season I was in by pining for the next one.

As I've grown older those sparkly things I've chased have changed shape, but they still lure me into some cosmic game of tag where recognition, success, affluence, and status are the advertised rewards. Not surprisingly, each rung of the ladder fails to deliver the happiness I expect it to, leaving me feeling disenchanted and defeated, hunting desperately for the next thing to work towards.

When I was single, I just wanted to be married, and once I had settled into wifedom, I just wanted to be a mom. When babies came along I couldn't wait for them to talk, and once they could, I longed for a moment of silence. I've wished away so many years I'll never get back in the endless pursuit of happiness and contentment.

CONFRONTING THE ILLUSION

As I arrived at each pin I had dropped on my life map - get a tattoo, launch a business, write a book - I found my eyes were already fixed on the next pin. There was so little of the delight I had expected to feel right where I was. Satisfaction was now off in the distance again, teasing me like an elusive mirage on the horizon.

Do more. Try harder. Become better. Then you'll be happy.

It wasn't that I couldn't achieve my goals, it was that even when I crushed them, they didn't seem to throw the party for me that I had expected. Where was the confetti and applause? But more importantly, where was that deep sense of satisfaction? Surely it should feel better than it did? And when it didn't, I'd move on to the next thing; head down, pedal to the metal, dreaming and pushing and hustling.

But those things that peddle neatly packaged happiness and contentment have one thing in common: they over-promise and under-deliver. They lure us in with the promise of pleasure and prosperity, but once we arrive and find we still feel empty, we forage for the next fix.

How much simple delight and beauty have I missed on the journey because my eyes have been so fixed on the destination? A destination that inevitably moves further out of reach as I arrive.

While I've come a long way, gleaning my value and significance from outside sources has always been a struggle for me. And I'm willing to bet I'm not the only one who gets beaten up on this very battlefield.

"Joy is not in things; it is in us"
Richard Wagner

DEFINING THE DIFFERENCE

If the acquiring, accomplishing or consuming of 'stuff' isn't what keeps us happy, how then do we foster a greater sense of happiness in our lives? A good starting point would be to acknowledge the difference between happiness and joy, and the way we experience the two.

Happiness is experienced when an external stimulus triggers it. Because it relies heavily on our circumstances being optimal, we tend to draw a direct line between happiness and pleasure. It provides fast, albeit temporary, pleasure - think candy bars, the honeymoon phase of marriage and Netflix marathons. Because the pleasure produced is temporary, we require another hit to sustain the endorphin-induced euphoria.

Joy on the other hand is cultivated within. If happiness is shallow and fleeting, easily found and easily lost, joy is deep and anchored, independent of our marital status, bank account or job title. It is experienced in the pleasure and the pain of the journey because it is not solely dependent on our circumstances.

If we hold external happiness in one hand and internal joy in the other, we'll notice that while happiness is louder and faster and shinier, joy is slower and weightier and more solid. The chasing of happiness is exhausting. The pursuit of joy is enriching and fulfilling. Hold them in your arms together and you've got a party worth attending.

The way the ancient Greeks defined happiness is very different from our understanding of it in the Western world. They defined it as "the joy you feel moving toward your potential". Rather than a destination we arrive at, it becomes a mode of travel and a lens through which we view life on the journey. Their understanding of happiness is rooted in joy.

Please understand that my intention is not to vilify happiness. It's a beautiful thing. But we cannot allow happiness to become something we burn ourselves out chasing, when it's a natural byproduct of choosing joy and cultivating it in our lives. Happiness is what leaks out of us when we intentionally choose joy in the everyday. When we choose to celebrate the small things. And when we acknowledge that, as in childbirth, even pain has a purpose and a role to play. It is here that we begin to understand how even when pleasure eludes us, we can still cultivate a deep sense of passionate joy and joy-filled passion.

While doing research for his book *The Happiness Advantage*, Shawn Achor[1] traveled to more than 50 countries and discovered some astounding things about the difference between joy-based and pleasure-based happiness. Shawn and his wife Michele met with and interviewed a broad spectrum of people across the world, from Swiss bankers to farmers in Zimbabwe. They found that the happiness factor - rooted in the ancient Greeks' understanding of happiness and more closely resembling joy - was far higher in the farmers who had lost everything than in the high-ups who hadn't received their bonus check for one week.

Achor found time and time again that those who had attempted to create happiness externally, and were living in plenty, were not nearly as joyful as those people who had fostered an internal sense of happiness, even while living in relative poverty. The latter group were able to find meaning and joy in their lives, in the midst of chaos and pain, because of three key factors:

• The power of their perspective (they were optimistic)
• Their ability to bounce back (they were resilient)
• The depth of their friendships (their 'social connection')

"We cannot change our past...we cannot change the fact that people will act in a certain way. We cannot change the inevitable. The only thing we can do is play on the one string we have, and that is our attitude...I am convinced that life is 10% what happens to me and 90% how I react to it."
Charles Swindoll

THE POWER TO CHOOSE

Another fascinating thing Achor discovered in his research was that there was a deep and abiding sense of joy in those who were generous with their time and resources. A concept we fondly refer to in our home as being "otherly".

The power of being otherly is what sparked the idea of the We ROAR Project[2] in early 2015. By leaning into the knowledge that I more quickly emerge from a funk when I shift my focus from myself and my insecurity, on to others and how I can encourage them, a simple revolution began. A movement of kindness that spread quickly around the United States, eventually popping up in South Africa, England and Australia.

The thing that amazes me most about the project was the fact that, had I chosen to stay in a place of self-pity and anxiety, it would never have happened, and the lives that have been touched through the simple dispersal of encouraging cards and acts of kindness would not have been impacted. It was a choice I had to make; either to stay inward focused and sad, or to turn outward, choosing joy and service instead.

It's always been about choice and it always will be, because we are created to change atmospheres and touch lives through the thoughtful use of our free will.

> "Joy is a net of love by which you can catch souls"
> *Mother Theresa*

Maybe negativity runs thick in your blood, but friend, it doesn't have to. Our ability to experience joy in life is not just genes and environment, you can choose to change. Happiness isn't something you inherit, it's something you cultivate. We'll dip into the neuroscience behind this a little more in the next chapter, but for now just know that you are powerful beyond anything you may have realized.

Happiness is a choice. Joy is a choice. Stress and anxiety and misery are also choices.

So choose well.

What you allow into your mind, your heart, and your schedule directly impacts your life. It effects your energy levels, your willingness to step out of your comfort zone to serve others, your ability to think and work creatively, and your general outlook on life. Choose joy in your media consumption, in your time management, and in your friendships. While being joyful is relatively easy for me (I guess I was named appropriately), my husband is what we affectionately refer to as 'joy-impaired'. He has to work extra hard to choose it, cultivate it and protect it. It is not his default-setting.

Our words are of the utmost importance; carrying in them the power to foster life or produce death. Think about it, God actually spoke the universe into existence. If we were made in His image, we've been given the ability to shape reality with what comes out of our mouths. Speak life, beloved. Over yourself, your dreams, your family and friends, and over your future.

In learning to watch what slips from our lips, we're more equipped and ready to guard our joy like the life-source it is.

While joy cannot actually be taken without our permission (it cannot be 'stolen' - we surrender it), it is up to us to guard it and avoid the things that threaten to suck it from our lives.

The never-ending ache for approval and the desperate need to be a part of something bigger than ourselves will never be met through material things, accomplishments, or other people. Yes, they're all good things, and they can add value to our lives, but they're not the source of our happiness. There's a reason joy is referred to in the Bible as a spiritual fruit; it develops in us slowly as we anchor our identity in truth, and plug our lives into the Source of that truth..

While being happy is a choice we can make every single day, it's ultimately the fruit of a deeper working. It's a byproduct of a life spent intentionally pursuing and choosing joy, and resting in the One who gives it.

Find joy in your life, grab it by the horns and refuse to let it go.

Fight for it and fiercely protect it.

Press into it, nurture it, cultivate it, and then, with everything you've got, spread it.

*"Joy does not simply happen to us.
We have to choose joy and keep choosing it"*
Henri Nouwen

DIG DEEPER ON PAGE 11
OF THE STUDY GUIDE

CHAPTER 2

A | ASK QUESTIONS

"Before I can tell my life
what I want to do with it,
I must listen to my life
telling me who I am"

PARKER PALMER

The seed-dream had poked its head out of the ground 2 years earlier. I think I want to write a book. The standard rush of excitement surged for a few days while the idea bounced around in my head. But then reality kicked in and I was reminded of all the reasons why it was a ridiculous notion.

After all it takes me hours to write a blog post. I have a terrible habit of editing while I write - which any author will tell you is creative suicide - and to add to this dilemma, what on earth did I think I could say that hadn't already been said in a million different ways. Who was I kidding?

But the feeling persisted and the little seedling continued

to poke its head above ground during seasons of inspiration, only to be withered again by practicality. I wasn't, after all, the writer in the family. My father, who had earned himself the affectionate title of "walking encyclopedia", was the ultimate pun-loving grammar guy and had co-authored a text book years earlier. He was author material. My older sister, well...she wrote and illustrated her first book at 6. While she had yet to formally publish anything, she was a writer. That girl can weave words together like nobody's business, inspiring belly laughter one minute and rattling you to the core with raw wisdom the next. Add to this the fact that my younger sister wrote and fully illustrated a delightful little children's book, which she then dedicated to our firstborn - still in utero at the time - at the ripe ol' age of 19.

Of the six members of my family, I was pretty sure I'd win the "least likely to write a book" nomination.

Over the course of the next few years I toyed with the idea several times, each time gaining a little more clarity and confidence on what it was I felt burdened to write about. As the seed grew and became harder to ignore, my "I think I want to write a book" graduated to "I'm going to write a book someday" and started to poke its little head above the surface.

In late February of 2014 I attended my first life coach training. Over the course of the weekend we learned the basics of coaching - what it is and maybe even more importantly, what it's not - and spent several hours practicing the art of asking great questions.

As the weekend drew to a close, I was running out of topics to get coached around. I had all but run out of things I wanted to work through, areas I needed clarity in, and battle plans I wanted to map out, when out of the blue the book idea emerged.

"I want to write a book", I blurted out, sitting across from

Ginger, an area pastor who was dipping her toes in the coaching pond for the first time too.

We only had twenty minutes, but what emerged during the course of that practice session was ground-breaking. It quite literally changed my life.

She didn't offer nuggets of wisdom that revolutionized the way I saw myself. She didn't tell me, "of course you can do it...go get 'em, tiger". Nor did she list all the reasons why I should just try. She simply asked questions. *Strategic, direct, clarifying questions that cut through all the unfounded muck of why I was convinced I wasn't a "writer" and cut to the heart of my desire to write.* Questions that stripped away all my apprehension, exposed all the lies I had believed, revealed how desperately I wanted to communicate hope through the written word, and set into motion an action plan that resulted in my first proof arriving in the mail 3 months later. It was absolutely mind-blowing.

Needless to say, I fell in love with coaching and the transformative power of asking the right questions.

"There are those that look at things the way they are, and ask why? I dream of things that never were, and ask why not?"
Robert F. Kennedy

Thought-provoking, open-ended questions have long been recognized as powerful tools to inspire creativity, promote self-awareness, clarify vision, reveal limiting-belief systems, and produce action. Coaching has been valued in the business world for many years, more recently showing up on the family and marriage front. I am absolutely delighted that churches are now embracing coaching as an effective means of empowering people to take responsibility for their lives. Jesus, after all, was the ultimate coach, asking life-changing questions and inspiring action throughout his ministry on earth.

Questions have a way of empowering us to take action like little else, while also providing clarity and focus. It's also easy to get caught up in a cycle of repetitive thinking, which ends up holding us captive to that thought. As we answer questions, we take the convoluted, jumbled mess of assumptions, misconceptions, hopes, fears and dreams, and we lay them on the table.

It never ceases to amaze me how this activity alone brings insight and inspires transformation. Once our thoughts are out on the table, we're able to pick through them in search of the gold, dismiss the junk and move ahead with a plan of action.

> *"You can tell whether a man is clever by his answers. You can tell whether a man is wise by his questions."*
> *Naguib Mahfouz*

NEUROPLASTICITY AND YOU

As we question why we actually believe the things we do - about ourselves or our circumstances - we're able to expose faulty thinking and limiting beliefs. This is huge in and of itself because of the power of our minds to create our reality. As airy-fairy as that may sound, hear me out.

There is reason we are told in Proverbs 4:23 to "above all else, guard your heart". Above *everything* else. In this scripture the word *heart* refers to your mind, will and emotions. Why should you guard them? Because "everything you do flows from it", the verse says. But we tend to get it backwards and guard all else *above* our hearts and minds. We put locks and alarm and secret pins on everything from our phones and cars to our homes, but we leave our minds open and vulnerable to the most destructive things.

And I would suggest that it's because we haven't a clue just how powerful our minds really are.

The writer was urging us to do what science is now confirming; your thought life matters. For too long, especially within the church culture, we've dismissed the notion that 'our thinking creates our reality' as new age mysticism. But scripture is filled with wisdom that neuroscience now backs up. 'As a man thinketh[3], so is he'.

Why does this matter, and why am I bringing this up now? Because the raw truth is, you will never accomplish what you don't believe you can, and you will not step into the life God has for you when you don't believe you're worthy of it.

What you believe about yourself, your future, and your God, will influence and shape your life more than anything else.

Because here's the deal; your thoughts are not just non-existent little vapors, here one moment, gone the next. They take up legitimate real estate in your brain[4]. Your brain doesn't shape your thoughts. Your thoughts shape your brain, which manifest in your life. Your thinking actually has an electro-chemical response in the brain, which basically means that what we end up dwelling on truly does impact our reality. What you focus on and feed, mentally, becomes how you flesh out your life.

Your thoughts either create healthy growth in your brain, like little branches of a tree, or unhealthy growth in the form of dark mangled branches. Not figuratively, but *literally*.

Let me map it out like this:
...what you think about creates physical responses in the brain, and determines how you feel.
...How you feel influences how you act in the moment.

...Moment by moment, your actions create habits,
...and your habits are what form your destiny.

To put it plainly; what you choose to *think* about
directly makes or breaks your life.

---

*"If I had to do it again, I'd ask more questions
and interrupt fewer answers"*
Robert Brault

I have utterly fallen in love with the science of our brains since stumbling upon the work of Dr. Caroline Leaf. She's a fiery South African, Jesus-loving neuroscientist, and her research is revolutionizing the way I think about thinking, as odd as that may sound, and how vigilantly I guard my thought life.

As she states[5], "75% to 95% of the illnesses that plague us today are a direct result of our thought life. What we think about affects us physically and emotionally. It's an epidemic of toxic emotions. The average person has over 30,000 thoughts a day. Through an uncontrolled thought life, we create the conditions for illness; we make ourselves sick! Research shows that fear, all on its own, triggers more than 1,400 known physical and chemical responses and activates more than 30 different hormones."

How does this effect our passion and our purpose? How does it not?

If we don't take responsibility for our thought-life, we reinforce deep ruts in the form of patterns in our daily life. It's incredibly hard to break out of those when we're stuck in our heads.

Strategic questions not only inspire creative problem-solving, they shatter those walls and invite us out of the cycle we didn't even realize we were stuck in. When it comes to passion, and figuring out what exactly it is we're passionate about, questions can reveal what our hobbies and propensities have been trying to tell us for years.

I never dreamed of being a writer, but I've always loved colorful words. Graphic design never featured on my radar as a teenager, but I've been obsessed with color, pretty fonts and layout since I was a young girl cutting up magazines to make a binder of pictures that made me happy. I never set out to be a speaker one day, but I was the kid who sat in the audience aching to be on stage doing something in the spotlight. The idea of owning my own business one day probably would have terrified me earlier on, but I just couldn't seem to bring myself to squeeze my dreams into somebody else's business hours. Everything in me pushed back against it.

I dabbled in retail, restaurant, radio and fitness, finding aspects I loved and loathed in each.

What did I want to be when I grew up? A marine biologist, a trapeze artist and a mermaid. Okay, I was 31 when I wanted to be a mermaid, and I blame this awkward confession entirely on the Denver Aquarium.

What did my soul long to do? Create, inspire, lead and love. Or more specifically; create freely, inspire authentically, lead bravely and love radically. It's really that simple.

As silly and sacrilegious as it may sound, I wholeheartedly believe the motivational sign that boldly states: you can be anything you want to be. I used to scoff at that theory, envisioning people trying desperately to turn into unicorns or candy bars, while spontaneously combusting instead. But the truth is: who really wants to be either? What is it that bubbles in your heart? Pay attention to that burning desire. I can almost guarantee you it's not to become an NBA star or the next president, but if it is, you're some kind of special and I'll be rooting for you!

As a mom to little ones, full of big dreams and unadulterated hope, I've come to realize afresh just how much power and responsibility God has actually given to us to make things happen. We like to palm it off on others, or place it all on God, but really it rests in our very capable hands and begins in our very powerful minds.

I do believe we can accomplish anything we set our minds to, mostly because I believe the things that consume our hearts and permeate our dreams point to a God-given calling on our lives. He planted it in us and it's our job to find it, feed it and nurture it. Unfortunately for us, it required getting out of our comfort zones and learning to dance with risk and failure.

> *"It's not that I'm so smart.*
> *But I stay with the questions much longer."*
> Albert Einstein

TIME TO SHAKE & WAKE

Take your time as you work through the questions on the next page (you'll find these and more in the study guide). Consider them a virtual coaching session of sorts. Don't rush. If you don't have time to tackle these now, schedule some quality time on your calendar to sit down with a pen and paper, delicious beverage in hand, and revisit them. Consider it an important date with you soul, and don't be late!

Pick each question up, noodle over it, massage it, flip it over, and then honestly respond. Because there's something incredibly powerful about writing out your thoughts, and then being able to revisit them at a later date, I would really encourage you to record them in a journal.

You'll find as you work your way through these questions that your answers may reveal themes throughout your life. It's often in hindsight that we identify these themes as the breadcrumbs along the path to the discovery of our passions and the fleshing out of our purpose.

QUESTIONS:

• What were your favorite things to do as a child?

• What do you love to do, despite the cost and in spite of the sacrifice it requires?

• What moves you deeply? (anger over injustice, sadness, joy over your convictions, etc.).

• What do you find people come to you for help with?

• What activity, when you're doing it, makes your spirit come alive?

• What hardship have you endured in your life that you now find yourself led to encourage others through?

• What irks you?

• What would you do if you weren't the least bit afraid?

You may be tempted to brush past the questions that beg you to examine what irks you or moves you in what might be perceived as a negative way. Intense, burning conviction is often the catalytic energy that has launched world-changing organizations and false-notion-squishing movements. Be it freedom, justice or equality, movements start with tapping into what moves us deeply. In fact, my first book was written with the passion and fire of a woman sick and tired of seeing sex distorted by the world, while being swept under the rug by Christians. I mounted my soapbox because of this deep conviction and it remains a topic I am passionate about.

You see, your anger, when stirred up over injustice or a dishonoring of important issues, can point you to your passion as clearly as something that elates you. And as Robert Madu[6] says, we are often called to correct the things we're criticizing, and tend to be "anointed for what annoys us".

As you work your way through these questions, it is my hope that you will see a theme emerging, leading to places where your answers overlap and reinforce each other?

Can you spot the common thread woven through your answers, and throughout your life? Grab on to this thread and follow it, it's going to lead you places, girlfriend!

*"Never give up on what you really want to do.
The person with big dreams is more
powerful than one with all the facts."*
H. Jackson Brown, Jr.

DIG DEEPER ON PAGE 13
OF THE STUDY GUIDE

CHAPTER 3

S | SILENCE COMPARISON

*"A flower does not think of
competing with the flower next to it,
it just blooms"*

ANON

It was a well-known fact in our home when we were growing up that my older sister was the artist. She could take a blank piece of paper and some colored pencils and within half an hour you'd have yourself a masterpiece.

Other kids would hover around and watch her draw at school because what emerged on her paper was always extraordinary. Awe and amazement were standard responses within a 5 foot radius when Sarah put pen to paper.

This had little to no impact on me when we were tiny tots. I didn't know any better. While she was creating little masterpieces, I spent most of my time in our swimming pool pretending to be a mermaid. In fact I was absolutely convinced I had sprouted gills and dreamed frequently that I could breathe under water.

When it came to putting pencil to paper, I loved to draw, but what I loved most was copying, tracing and sketching still life. I needed to see something before I could create it. My creativity seemed to require external inspiration and guidance and wasn't very original. Sarah, on the other hand, could have a perfectly blank slate and what would appear before our eyes was unique, unlike anything we'd seen before...colorful and whimsical. I always envisioned the inside of her head looking like scenes from the Robin Williams movie, What Dreams May Come.

She did her thing and I happily did mine.

It wasn't until we were a little older that I thought to compare our gifts and talents.

When we were 8 and 10, respectively, mom roped us into a drawing competition in the hopes that one of us would win the prized bus tickets. With all of our family still living in South Africa, we made at least one trip from Windhoek, Namibia back to Cape Town, South Africa every year. It was a long, hot 15-hour endeavor across the country, a journey typically made in our underwear and without seat-belts.

Enter: the Mainliner. This luxury bus service, while pretty costly for a young family of 6, was a brilliant solution to an excruciatingly long drive. It was air-conditioned, had bathrooms on board, and made the excursion more of a journey to be enjoyed than a trek to be endured.

All we had to do to enter was draw a picture of a Mainliner bus. No problemmo. I whipped that bad boy out. Being an accomplished perfectionist (ahem) I've always been good with shapes, so my wheels were adequately circular, and the stripes on the side of the bus were precise. My sun was decidedly yellow and round and the smiling faces I drew in each little window were...well, sweet and simple.

My sister's entry was anything but simple. She had sketched out Namibia's signature sand dunes, shading the sky above into blazing sunset perfection. I'm not sure whether it was the exquisite little gemsbok she drew in the distance, or the detail with which she crafted the bus that convinced the judges, but they were convinced alright...that she had cheated and that a parent had drawn it for her. And I won the competition. 6 tickets from Windhoek to Cape Town, baby!

Boy, was my sister mad! Her masterpiece had lost to my childlike drawing because the judges couldn't wrap their heads around a young child creating what she had.

I don't know if this was the first time I had looked at my offering, then over at hers, and finally back at mine - painfully aware of the discrepancy between the two - but it is one of the first times I remember the deflating effect of comparison sneaking into my creative processes.

> *"Comparison is the thief of joy"*
> *Theodore Roosevelt*

LOSING OURSELVES

It was as if someone had traded in my little work lamp for an unforgiving flood light. My focus had begun to shift from enjoyment of my own work and on to the people around me. What were *they* doing, and how did mine compare?

It's interesting, as I look back, how quickly I started to categorize people and place them into their appropriate compartments. The haves and the have-nots, creatively speaking. The box that defined creative expression got smaller and smaller, making it harder and harder to fit into.

My big sister clearly could draw and paint and create, so she was an artist. Which meant I was obviously *not*.

And she would devour books, late at night, under the covers with a flashlight. She loved words. Reading and writing came naturally to her. She, along with my equally book-savvy dad, were the readers and writers in the family. In comparison, I was neither.

If someone possessed a quality that was noticed and celebrated - be it physical beauty or a particular skill - and what I possessed didn't resemble theirs, then I just didn't have it. It was a simple, deficit-driven process of elimination.

She's really pretty, and looks like that. I don't look anything like her, so this obviously means I'm not pretty.

She's crazy smart. My mind doesn't work the way hers does, nor do I have that amount of schooling, which can only mean I'm not smart.

Talented. Spiritual. Wealthy. Funny. Insert your descriptor of choice. My raging insecurity was quick to whisper, "well, you got the short end of the stick, didn't you?".

While this very black-and-white method of categorizing may work with sorting farm animals, it's an incredibly destructive way to think about ourselves or others. It in no way honors the incredible creativity and uniqueness with which we've been made.

I hear it all the time from women; *oh, I'm not creative*. But what they're really saying is "I'm not creative like so-and-so". Our understanding of the word 'creative' has become so shallow and narrow. What we seem to forget is that we were created in the image of God, the Creator, and so we have it woven into our DNA to be creative. We are *all* creative. *You are creative*. It's just that our methods and expressions are so very different - and this is no accident. After all, how monotonal our chorus would be if we all held the same note or had the same creative expression.

"Why fit in when you were born to stand out?"
Dr. Seuss

The effect of limiting our view of creativity to only what we see on Pinterest or the Instagram feed displayed by a select few is as destructive as whittling down our definition of beauty to a minuscule list of definitions, dimensions and air-brushed curves. In the same way the "real beauty" movement is rising up to speak truth and smash false ideals, we need to reclaim our creativity and celebrate a broader definition of it - without comparison.

STAY IN YOUR LANE

It's still a thrill to watch my older sister create. She can take the most basic of ingredients - be it fresh food or beach pebbles - and create something extraordinary. She was, and still is, a creative genius.

These days, as the mother of two young girls, her mediums may have changed slightly, but the creative brilliance remains. She can take a granny smith apple, two grapes, a carrot and a toothpick and carve out the cutest little tree frog you've ever seen. The children's birthday parties this woman throws will blow your mind. And not one ounce of it is to show-off, it is pure enjoyment for her.

The art she creates in her garden is mesmerizing. From the multi-tiered raised beds, overflowing with herbs and berries, to the 'princess and the pea' mannequin she hand-painted and placed in the vegetable garden, complete with chicken wire skirt for peas to climb.

I remember watching her garden emerge that first season after we both had moved into new homes. Every time we visited it was more vibrant and alive than before. It seemed effortless to her, therapeutic even. So I went home and started plotting out my garden. Excited and motivated at first, the enthusiasm faded as the reality of daily watering and weeding settled in, and as I started to lose fruit of my reluctant labor to blight, bugs and beasties.

Long story short, I hated it. I tried again for two more years, hoping something might be different, but there was little I enjoyed about gardening after the initial digging and planting process. I was overtaken by guilt. Isn't this what domestically-savvy women do? They garden...and they love it, dog-gone it. What was wrong with me? It didn't help that this realization was sinking in around the same time Pinterest was exploding. Having shared pictures of my cute dirt-encrusted kids and growing garden on my blog added a pressure to deliver results. If I fail at this, or admit defeat, it will mean public defeat. Besides, how could I fail at something so simple and practical...and trendy.

While it took me a couple of years to realize and accept this, it was incredibly liberating when I realized that simply because something was someone else's "thing", didn't mean it had to be mine. In fact, going against the grain and trying to make it mine typically produced more anxiety than red peppers.

So hear me when I say: I don't like gardening. Not.one.bit. The thought of canning makes me want to cry. I cook because it keeps my people alive. There. I said it. And boy does it feel good.

"How much time he gains who does not look to see what his neighbour says or does or thinks, but only at what he does himself, to make it just and holy."
Marcus Aurelius

We all have areas of passion and expertise we flourish in - If you think you're exempt from this, you just haven't found yours yet (refer back to the previous chapter). They are like lanes we travel in. It's where the saying, "stay in your lane" comes from. While I don't like the idea of being hemmed in and limited to one lane, I do think there's tremendous wisdom in staying focused on our areas of strength and not veering off into someone else's lane. While it's fine to experiment and explore, it's important to realize that no one will ever do things - even the same things - in exactly the same way you do; with your flavor, your style and your voice. The same is also true of others. When we look over and covet their lane, we're forgetting it's a package deal. We can't see through their lens, bring their experiences and unique stories to the table, or work within their cluster of strengths and gifts.

In the same way it's dangerous to take our eyes off the road in front of us while we're driving, when we allow our creative eyes to wander over to other lanes to inspect what other people are doing, we risk running ourselves off the road altogether. Not only is it dangerous to our emotional and cognitive health, it's also destructive in the sense that when we magnify what others are doing, we tend to minimize what we've got going on in our own lane. And in turn it's incredibly wasteful of our own precious creative energy.

Where comparison takes root, coveting and competition grows. Insecurity runs rampant, giving way to jealousy, shame and ingratitude. And nothing creative is ever born in that place.

> We too often silence and stuff what we can do
> because of what we feel we can't do.

How wise it would be for us to simply throw our hands up and, as Jess Connolly[7] so wisely says, take ourselves out of the race. With a gracious 'thanks, but no thanks' to comparison-based competition, might we find a fresh love for our 'thing' when we're perfectly content to not be the best. What sweet life and freedom might we find in our work once the urge to compare has been removed.

I love what Brené Brown has to say about unexpressed creativity. She explains that it is "not benign - it metastasizes. It turns into grief, rage, judgment, sorrow, shame". Untapped creativity will wreak havoc in our lives and the lives of others, not because it doesn't want to come out, but because when we suppress it for one reason or another, it tends to fester.

I will never forget being out on a run one crisp Autumn morning when I heard a surprising story about Hitler on the podcast I was listening to. Believe it or not, young Adolf dreamed of becoming a professional artist. He created hundreds of works of art in his youth, painting everything from scenery and buildings to Mary and baby Jesus. It is said that he even carried his paints with him while serving in World War I, painting farmer's houses during his down time.

This charismatic leader was incredibly creative, but something profound had shifted and started to back up the flow which eventually poisoned the expression. His dreams of becoming a professional painter had been shattered when he was rejected by the Academy of Fine Arts in Vienna, not once, but twice. Not surprisingly, his autobiography, published in the 1920s and entitled Mein Kampf, translates "My Struggle".

For whatever reason it may be that we don't allow our unique creative expression out to play, or give it the freedom it requires - whether it's because it doesn't look the way we think it should look, or because someone in a position of authority has decided it doesn't make the cut – the inevitable loss will be felt as a weight that holds us back from realizing our God-given potential. And this loss will always impact lives beyond our own.

> "We are born makers. We move what we're learning
> from our heads to our hearts through our hands"
> *Brené Brown*

As long as I am threatened by other women - their gifts, their strengths or their confidence - and compare my offering to theirs, I will refuse to celebrate or champion their journey. Instead I pull my signature 'anemone' move by turning inward, missing out on the opportunity to genuinely connect with them, and breaking the link of greater community.

I've come to realize in recent years just how much of a problem this is for me, and how destructive and community-squelching this kind of jealousy can be. This mentality breeds fear and feeds the pervasive misunderstanding that if you do well it means I can't, or that if you move into town with all your fabulousness, there won't be room for me to do my own fabulous thing...so why bother.

The world isn't only big enough for all we are and all we uniquely have to offer; it is better for it when we do.

Communities come to life, creativity is expressed, needs get met, and the canvas of broad human creativity becomes more vibrant than ever as we boldly step up and bring that thing we have to offer the world and lay it on thick.

"We won't be distracted by comparison if we're captivated with purpose"
Bob Goff

DIG DEEPER ON PAGE 16
OF THE STUDY GUIDE

CHAPTER 4

S | SURROUND YOURSELF

"If you want to go fast, go alone.
If you want to go far, go together"

AFRICAN PROVERB

Women can be scary. I know. There's nothing like entering the rocky terrain of motherhood to remind you how opinionated, cluster-hungry and judgmental women can be. We like to call them the mommy-mafia. And I used to champion a local chapter.

Insecurity and fear fuel the division. Fear that if you do it differently from me, and believe you're right, then that makes me wrong. So I'll judge you before you have the chance to judge me, which makes me feel better about my decisions, and because, Lord knows, I can't stand being wrong.

And then there's the fear of being found out as having no clue what I'm doing. Because I *don't*. So the line I draw in the sand, between the illusion of my imagined perfection and your supposed hot mess, just keeps my hot messiness under wraps.

Oh yes. There's nothing quite like motherhood to expose our deep need to belong, be loved and feel accepted. And the ugliness that emerges when those needs are compromised. It doesn't help that our bodies have been shredded and we don't sleep well for the first few years. But that's a different book.

MADE FOR EACH OTHER

There is an extraordinary gardening method I stumbled upon a couple of years ago, while gathering illustrations for a talk on the power of community, called 'companion planting'.

According to Native American legend, the Iroquois found that when they planted specific vegetables together, in close proximity, they were healthier and more productive than when planted apart. This was especially true of corn, beans and squash.

Planted on a mound, they discovered that the corn provided a natural pole for the beans to climb, while the network of bean vines fortified the stalk of the corn. The beans fixed the nitrogen levels in the soil, while the squash spread out and created a living mulch of sorts over the soil, keeping moisture in and weeds down. The prickly vines of the squash also helped to deter little paws from reaching the beans and corn.

The Native Americans that mastered this planting technique, reaped the trifecta in vegetable harvest, and dubbed it the "three sisters". And it's easy to see why. They didn't thrive in spite of their differences, but because of them.

In the same way certain plants do better in companionship with others, similarly we were designed to grow in close community with each other.

There is, deeply etched into the core of every human being, a need for community and a desire to belong. We emerge from the womb on a hunt for "our people", and we will stop at nothing to find them. This explains why so many struggling, insecure teens will end up compromising their values and tracking with the wrong crowd. If that colorful crowd meets an innate need that's not being met at home, risky as it may be to their health and future, just hand them their membership card, because they're in.

We will do virtually anything to fit in. It's hard-wired into our DNA. We were created for community; to quite literally 'do life together'.

Living the life you were created for, full of passion and purpose - in the midst of community - is a full contact sport. It will not be without difficulty or heartache. After all, anytime you have more than one human in any given space for an extended period of time, you have the potential recipe for conflict. Just look at marriage.

But when we learn to handle each other with grace, intentionally choosing not to allow our feathers to be too easily ruffled, while keeping the big picture in mind, even conflict becomes a powerful avenue for growth, development and depth. To avoid close community in the name of conflict-avoidance creates a far greater deficit than what we feel we might experience simply dealing directly with drama. While I am emotionally allergic to drama, and do love my alone time, I crave authentic community and know my life is far richer because of it.

FIND YOUR TRIBE

I have been incredibly blessed to 'do life' alongside a group of amazing women over the past fifteen years.

When I first got married and was navigating life as a new bride, those girlfriends who were in those unchartered waters with me were such a source of encouragement and support. I needed to hear that I wasn't the only one struggling with selfishness and an ever-growing need for good conflict resolution skills.

As a new stay-at-home mom, drowning in diapers, cheerios and tiny toenail clippings, those fresh loin-fruit producing friends were my saving grace. Balm for my weary momma soul. I needed to know I wasn't the only sleep-deprived woman with leaky-boobs and misplaced libido.

When I wrote my first book, I clung to my writer friends. It gave me such hope to know I wasn't the only one suffering from writer's block, verbiage-inadequacy-syndrome and a severe lack of clean laundry.

As I've grown spiritually, I have treasured the insight and camaraderie that's come from gathering with other women seeking to stretch and deepen their faith. I've ached to know I'm not alone in my struggles with doubt and defeat and trust.

When I first assumed the role of LEOW, or 'law enforcement officer's wife', it was calming for my nerves to have other wives with whom to process concerns and fears. Not to mention health insurance woes. How exactly do you send the love of your life out into an angry world each day, knowing it could be the last time you see them alive? And while this is true for every human, no matter their vocation, LEOWs simply have more obvious reminders of this daily reality.

Every hat we wear and every role we play through the various seasons of life offer opportunities to find our tribe along the way.

You see, one of the most beautiful things about surrounding yourself with community is the resounding, "me too!" that echoes when you're together. Something shifts in the atmosphere when we take off our masks, let down our hair, and link arms. When we vulnerably share our successes and struggles, and our findings and failures.

The healing power of sojourning as a tribe is found as we bring both the beautiful and the broken parts of our souls to the table and breathe. We exhale loneliness and fear and inhale encouragement and hope.

It is here that we are reminded that we're not alone in our struggles, that we're not naive in our searching, and that support is just an arm's length away.

NOT AN ISLAND

I had forgotten about the power of those circles until I hit a low point last year. While my hubby and I are regularly plugged into several relational circles in our community and beyond, when I stepped out into something new and somewhat scary, I quickly became aware of my painful lack of tribal support there.

With my kids back in school for the Fall, I was again in the studio, doing what I love to do; create. Whether it's writing or painting or coaching or developing conference material, my heart is happiest when I'm marrying my passion for creativity with my drive to empower and equip others. And yet I felt heavy. I found myself walking into the studio - a space that I simply adore - with an unmistakable void in my heart. I couldn't put my finger on the cloud that hovered above me, but it absolutely baffled me that I would feel such an empty ache when I was doing what I love to do.

And then it hit me; I was desperately lonely. While I enjoy my alone time, and need solitude to focus and work, I am undeniably a people-loving extrovert. I needed fellowship and didn't have a clue how to fill that void without filling my schedule with time-sucking appointments and lunch dates. I joined a young professionals network, but that didn't seem to remedy the ache. Life as a solopreneur was just different.

In the Spring of the following year a woman reached out to me. We had been introduced by a mutual friend a few years earlier and, thanks to the wonders of social networking, had stayed in touch and collaborated on a few creative projects. She wanted to know whether I'd be interested in accompanying her to a weekly gathering of female business women, and while I was mildly terrified and felt out of my league, I went anyway. What if I didn't fit in? What if they didn't like me, or found me annoying? What if I wasn't professional or talented or stylish enough to be a contributing member of this group? And what if being in the presence of #girlboss success made my #wannabe status painfully obvious?

Nerve-wrecking as that first meeting may have felt at the time, it was one of the best decisions I have made for my business ventures, my creative spirit, and my tribe-loving heart.

Let me tell you, these women...they're my people. We dream out loud together, we wrestle with concepts, we brain storm, we bounce ideas off each other, and we generously share resources and expertise. We support each other and celebrate one another. We even occasionally cry together.

They are beautiful, brilliant, bold and brave. And each

one has brought a unique flavor to the tossed salad of our weekly passion potluck.

Making the twenty-mile trip into town and spending ninety minutes with these women every week has been the best investment I've made in my future for a long time. I didn't realize how desperately I needed a "work circle" in my life until the presence of that void in my day became an open wound in my soul.

"Whatever you do in life, surround yourself with smart people who'll argue with you"
John Wooden

The people you choose to walk through life with - and it is a choice - influence the journey in many ways. They impact the culture and atmosphere, the speed, and the direction. Kathy Ireland, a retired model and successful entrepreneur, separated people into two groups; anchors and engines. And while I fondly refer to my husband as the rock that anchors my balloon, she's not referring to anchors in a grounding way, but in a dead-weight, keep-you-stuck and hold-you-back kind of way.

Because the people you allow in your inner circle effect your life, whether you like it or not, this chapter would be incomplete without a little chat around the topic of boundaries.

BOUNDARY LINES

I love the way Danny Silk[8] describes boundaries. Picture an aerial view of your home with a series of concentric circles around it; the small inside circle nestled inside your bedroom, and the largest one extending out past your driveway. We have a long driveway which affords us plenty of circles (it is alright; jealousy is allowed here).

As you mentally work through the list of people closest to you - not necessarily those you have the closest relationships with, but those who have the most influence in your life - decide which ring would be healthiest for them to be in.

For instance, there are some people who simply drive by our home, we smile and wave, but that is the extent of our connection. We'll call them the 'village people'. Feel free to mentally assign appropriate costumes to the folk in this category while humming "YMCA". I won't judge you.

Then there are 'driveway people'. We all have them. We recognize the fact that they are in our lives (due to familial connection or workplace necessity), and we go out of our sacred space (our home, representing an inner circle) to meet them. This relationship involves some distance, whether liked by them or not, and is a healthy boundary for the relationship in terms of time investment and proximity.

There are 'front porch people'. We spend more time with them, enjoy their company and there's a level of comfort here, with them on our turf. The 'living room people' are those we have intentionally welcomed into our lives. The close relationship is mutually beneficial and healthy, and we share a vibrant connection with these people. They would be like the 12 disciples to Jesus.

Bedroom people are those closest to our hearts, our inner circle. This would be Peter, James and John for Jesus. There's an intimacy, if you will, in our relationship that feeds and nurtures the spirit and soul. These people are your spouse and closest friends. Although only your spouse gets to bounce on your bed. But all of that is in my *other* book (wink, wink).

We use this analogy a lot in mentoring couples because it visually enables them to process through where they're placing their spouse, family members and friends. It helps them more practically manage those relationships that are toxic to their marriage. While we can't always cut people out of our lives, we can invest in them, at a distance, for 5 minutes in the driveway, rather than 5 hours in the living room.

John Rohn worded it this way; "we are the average of the five people we spend the most time with". He hit the nail on the head. You become like who you spend the most time with. Which also provides a strong case for intentionally pursuing a healthy spiritual walk with your Creator. Who better to become more like than Him?

HEMMED IN

In each area of your life; physical, spiritual, relational and vocational, make sure you're surrounding yourself with people equally as committed to each goal as you are, and then some.

...If you want to be a better wife, surround yourself with women who passionately love their husbands and are committed to their marriages.

...If you want to be a better mom, surround yourself with women who authentically and intentionally parent with firm boundaries and a grace-soaked heart.

...If you want to grow in your spiritual life, surround yourself with women who are hungry for more intimacy with God and work to cultivate audacious faith in their everyday lives.

...If you want to get physically healthy, surround yourself with people who recognize the value of what they put in their mouths and the effects of how they treat their bodies.

...If you want to grow as an entrepreneur, surround yourself with women who dream big, work hard, share resources, and who believe in the power of the collective.

Core values, passion and drive are more contagious than we realize.

While we'll dig more deeply into the topic of mentoring in the Overflow & Input chapter (under the Purpose section), I cannot stress enough how important it is that you surround yourself with great people, specifically women. Get them in the living room of your heart. They will add fuel to your life's passion, and remind you of your mission when the going gets tough. These friendships are worth their weight in gold.

"Call it a clan, call it a network, call it a tribe, call it a family. Whatever you call it, whoever you are, you need one".
Jane Howard

DIG DEEPER ON PAGE 18
OF THE STUDY GUIDE

| | INSPECT YOUR ROOTS

"If an egg is broken by outside
force, life ends. If broken by inside
force, life begins. Great things
always begin from inside."

JIM KWIK

Several years ago, while my husband was laid off and I was 7 months pregnant with our second child, we packed up our lives into a 10x20 shipping container and moved in with my parents. While we only intended to stay for a month or two, it was almost a year before we were able to move out again on our own.

My parents graciously offered us their master-suite and moved themselves into the finished basement. My baby sister, almost 9 years younger than I am, was down the hall. It was a full house and it was glorious. But it was also challenging and character-building, this whole close-proximity thing. While sharing a bedroom with a 2-year-old and a newborn was a feat all on its own, the anticipation of one day again owning and decorating my own space kept me hopeful. The creative potential of a whole home to myself had me doodling and dreaming my way through those long months of community living.

With the discovery of our first pregnancy, a couple of years earlier, we had purchased an all neutral nursery set. Being the frugal gal that I am, I wasn't interested in decking out the place in pink and purple, only to redo the nursery if our second child turned out to be boy. So when we discovered a boy would indeed be emerging next, I breathed a satisfied sigh at my neutral selection...and then went to town buying cute girly things for our daughter's "big girl" bedroom. Gingham lined baskets in shades of pink, purple polka-dot lampshades, glittered owl coat hooks, cute wooden artwork, you name it. I ferreted away the growing stash of pretty stuff I'd accumulated with the rest of our storaged stuff, awaiting our son's arrival and the big bedroom graduation that would accompany my husband's return to work.

Two months turned into four, and four months became eight, and before we knew it, we'd had our lives packed away in storage for almost a year.

But then moving day finally arrived. My hubby had been recalled, we'd found a home closer to his work, and the storage container had been scheduled for drop-off. The wait was over and the anticipation was intoxicating.

I remember the day we moved in like it was yesterday. It was May 11th, 2010, and I was giddy. To have our clothes, our furniture, our tchotchkes...in our house.

The delight quickly turned to devastation as we opened the doors and started to unload the unit. I'm not sure what gave it away first; the musty smell, or the gradually damper boxes, but by the time we were halfway in, we knew something was horribly wrong. We were beginning to discover moldy furniture, swollen cracked wood, rusty lampshades, and totes upon totes of color-streaked, soaking wet clothes.

Apparently a tiny leak in the roof, over in the far right corner, had allowed just enough water in to dissolve my excitement.

A box stacked on top - just beneath the hole - had filled with rainwater, smashing the box beneath it with its weight, and shattering the wine glasses in the box below that. It was a domino effect of destruction. Even our dining room table had dark mold growing on the surface.

When I got to the boxes that held Alathea's beautiful, brand-new bedroom decor, I crumpled and wept so hard that I dry-heaved. 11 months of excitement now shattered, emerged in a groan so ugly that my husband ushered me in and away from the semi-terrified delivery men.

UNCOVERED

What had held so much promise and potential on the outside, carried only heart-ache and disappointment beneath the surface.

We often get caught up in the glamor of external things and forget the importance of surveying what lies below the surface, in unseen places.

We want the medal, but don't want to put in the time training for and enduring the marathon.

We want big, juicy fruit, but preferably without the labor. It just isn't fun having to get our hands dirty putting in the time tending to the roots that feed said fruit.

I ooh and aah over the beauty of others' projects and words and accomplishments, but forget the work they've put in behind the scenes, when no one was watching or applauding. The long nights extending into the wee hours, the months when it seemed no one cared, the many long years of work that led up to their "overnight success".

We rarely acknowledge the price people have paid to be where they are, for "success" always comes at a cost.

While we see and celebrate what happens above the ground, we need to understand that what happens beneath the surface is of far greater importance. While not always immediately evident, the health - or lack thereof - beneath will eventually come to light above.

What is grown and cultivated underground in the dark will ultimately be reflected above the surface, in the light; in our lives or on our limbs.

THE GROUNDED PLATFORM

Have you seen the little cartoon that has circulated on social media of the two rabbits holding their carrots? The proud little guy on the right is smugly gripping the leafy plumage that towers out of the ground and over his head, while the little dude on the left is standing there, slightly intimidated, holding his little cluster of carrot fern.

From where they're standing, the bunny on the right is far more impressive than the other. But what's happening under their feet is what speaks volumes. While they're holding onto - and assessing - what's growing above ground, what's developing beneath the soil is quite the opposite. And far more important. The cocky bunny has a tiny little carrot beneath the massive explosion of foliage, while the slightly intimidated rabbit on the left has grown a large, healthy looking carrot beneath his unimpressive greenery.

We too often measure things by the way they look, rather than what they're made of. We evaluate at the surface level when what sits above the surface is often a poor reflection of what's going on behind the scenes.

> We make assumptions about others' success based on the height of their branches, rather than the depth of their roots.

I am so guilty of paying more attention to the ostentatious plumage than to the not-so-obvious root system, forgetting that what is invested in the unseen places will always show up above ground. Eventually. What is neglected beneath the surface will manifest there too. While we can shape and prune what grows above, we will not see substantial, genuine growth without investing in and nurturing the roots. It is of utmost importance that we tend to those tender unseen places first.

While I'm often tempted to neglect the inside in favor of pampering the outside, I distinctly recall a period where I wrestled especially hard with it. I so desperately wanted to keep growing my business, ministry and platform that I focused all my attention on what others could see, while neglecting the root system of all three. With my first book out and some level of momentum building, I wanted to stand on my tippy-toes and pick ripe fruit, not get down on my knees and get my hands dirty in the soil of soul work. I had already done so much deep heart-stuff over the decade before, which had been poured vulnerably into that book, surely I could stop now?

I struggled with fierce jealousy toward others who seemed to be going viral, spreading their branches at neck-breaking speed, resenting the fact that my business and platform weren't growing faster. Slow and steady runs the race, they say. But "bring on the miracle-grow" was my anthem.

At a particularly low point, during which I considered throwing in the towel and walking away, I realized in how precarious of a spot I had put myself. I was headed for disaster. I had focused so much on manicuring and styling the few branches I already had, while starving the only thing I truly had any control over; my root system.

Things came to a head in late 2014 and I knew it was time to get my hands dirty.

My theme word that year was *'rooted'*. I believe God was inviting me to examine my roots; what type of soil was I allowing myself to grow in, what was nourishing and sustaining my business, and would it be enough to anchor me when the storms of life arose? The answer was a simple "no". I had spread myself a mile wide but grown only an inch deep, taking refuge in the little pot of my comfort zone where I was fast becoming root-bound.

While it was hard, messy work, I am so thankful I took the time to dig into those tender, twisted places. While I may have looked perfectly put together on the outside, there was decay happening beneath the surface that was slowly working its way through. Deep systemic damage takes a while to show up on the surface, but it's there if you take the time to look.

"Confidence on the outside begins
by living with integrity on the inside"
Brian Tracy

I had my work cut out for me; untangling faulty belief-systems, pruning unhealthy stragglers, weeding out lies I had believed, and finding healthier, more vibrant soil to flourish in.

I needed to take that time to securely establish myself in what mattered, even if it meant no one was applauding, liking or following the progress. I sensed God reminding me, "be faithful with what I've put in your hand, and I'll honor what I've put in your heart".

Over the course of that next year, as my focus shifted to what grew beneath the surface[9], I started to intentionally feed the areas that were starving, forcing myself out of my comfort zone and networking with other creative professionals who longed to use their influence the same way I did.

While it may not have looked like it on the surface, much was happening below. There was such tremendous growth in my mind and heart that year, along with several significant paradigm shifts. What was poured into my roots during that season has started to show up on my branches, and the new growth is beyond exciting.

Had I grown above ground as quickly as I had wanted to in years prior, I would not have survived. I simply didn't have what it took to sustain and anchor substantial branch growth, and I would have ended up on my face, neglected roots in the air. My husband tried to call me on it several times, anxious that I would crash and burn, but I always had a reason for why I was operating the way I was.

My roots are more substantial now than what spreads out above the surface, serving as a more grounded, well established anchor for those turbulent times, and reaching out to draw nourishment from wiser, healthier sources (we'll dig into this in chapter 12).

TIME TO TEND

I love the visual reminder provided by the Chinese Bamboo[10] tree that grows in the Far East. For the first few years, water and fertilize it as you might, it doesn't seem to respond. It just sits there in the ground, an unassuming little seedling. To the casual passerby, it would seem it's not interested in growing big and strong at all. But it's quite the opposite actually. Underground the roots are taking shape. All of its energy is going to establishing a network of roots, preparing a foundation for what's to come. In its fifth year it goes bonkers. That unassuming little bamboo stalk shoots for the sky and grows over eighty feet in six weeks.

> *"Don't get confused between what people say you are and who you know you are"*
> *Oprah*

An addiction to the approval of others can drive us into performance mode, where we're tempted to hang plump fruit we have manufactured, rather than cultivated, on our limbs for all the world to see. This is especially tempting on social media platforms like Instagram and Facebook where everyone presents their edited, well-lit best.

We buy into the lie that our value and self-worth is attached to how well we perform, and how loudly others respond to our performance, while slowly but surely, authenticity is lost. Once that mask is in place, it's very hard to remove it. Not only is the illusion unsustainable, we inevitably set ourselves up for disaster.

There is a real danger in not being firmly grounded, especially in a tech savvy world where a good designer can throw together a hip website and make you look like the best thing since sliced bread. Where titles like, "international best-seller and "world-renowned expert" get whipped out like fortunes from a cookie.

While it's tempting to present air-brushed perfection and lofty self-proclamation, we run the risk of growing externally (above the ground) faster than internally (beneath the ground). When our branches reach out further than our root systems can support, we will inevitably fall apart. We can all think of people who rose to fame fast, and fizzled from the lime-light even faster.

Being willing to take the mask off and get our hands dirty, discovering what we're made of, will cost us time and energy. It takes incredible bravery, humility and grace, and a willingness to be seen for who we are. But the cost of not taking the time to examine our roots is more costly by far.

While our fruit proudly displays our charisma, our roots reveal our character. Charisma may be useful in expressing our passion in colorful display, but our character will always be the steady driving force that sustains our passion through famine or feast.

"The Lord does not look at the things people look at. People look at the outward appearance, but the Lord looks at the heart."
1 Samuel 16:7

DIG DEEPER ON PAGE 20
OF THE STUDY GUIDE

CHAPTER 6

O | OWN YOUR STORY

*"You either walk inside your story
and own it or you stand outside your
story and hustle for your worthiness"*

BRENE BROWN

It was almost midnight when my husband responded to the cali. White male, gunshot wound to the chest. He was found by a driver who had noticed his unattended car on the side of the road, and then stumbled upon his body beside the vehicle. Alongside two shotgun shells. The first to make sure everything worked, the second a desperate attempt to end the pain.

The bullet had torn through his diaphragm, breaking every single rib and blowing out the back between shoulder blade and arm pit. My husband spent the next several minutes with his hands cupped inside his chest cavity, holding organs in place and packing gauze to stop the bleeding.

"You're going to be okay, man. You are alive...you still have breath in your lungs, and you're going to pull through. You hear me? God has a purpose for your life, it's not over yet. Stay with me...stay with me, man!"

It wasn't long after this bloody encounter that I was rolling over to do the signature police wife bed-sweep for evidence of my hubby's sleeping body. He wasn't home and it was several hours past the end of his shift. A simple message let me know he was at the hospital with a young man who had attempted suicide. He's right where he needs to be, I remember thinking, before I dozed off again.

It was a night neither man will forget, and one that earned my husband a life-saving award.

Yesterday marked two months since the incident. As he sat in his favorite recliner, cup of tea in hand and download of the day taking place, my hubby stopped and looked at me. "I called him today". This young man, a husband and daddy to two little girls, had since endured several long surgeries to repair tissue and reconstruct damaged organs.

My husband stopped short and looked at me, eyes damp and wide in an attempt to not send tears rolling. "He thanked me, babe. He said he remembered every word I said while we were waiting for the ambulance. Every word. And that it meant so much to him. He gets that it's a total miracle that he's alive".

Despite the damage done to his chest cavity and surrounding tissue, his heart and lungs were untouched. By all standards, he should be dead today. But he's not. He has breath in his lungs and a story to tell. And knowing that makes all the difference.

"I don't think of all the misery,
but of the beauty that still remains".
Anne Frank

You have a story to tell. As do I. We all do.

It may not be an epic saga of gunshot wound survival, but there's a story wrapped into your days and it's aching to be shared. If you have breath in your lungs today it is because God has breathed it into you, and it's your responsibility to spend your days breathing out your part of that story.

What's your story? Have you ever sat with that question long enough to figure out the answer?

There are tales of bravery and accomplishment, punctuated with paragraphs of difficulty and pain. There are chapters that tell of loneliness endured, heart-break experienced, and resilience developed. And of a million tiny moments that together paint a picture of everyday courage, perseverance and the power of simply being pesent. Pages upon pages of just.showing.up. There are stories of lies believed and identities stolen, of betrayal and healing and growth. Of redemption. Oh, sweet redemption.

But our gaze wanders and our focus shifts, and as we examine the polished appearance of others' stories, comparison hijacks the raw beauty of our own story, and we tuck them out of sight.

OUT OF HIDING

You have a story, friend, and your story matters. You are not here by accident and every one of your days is held carefully in the hands of the One who wove you together in your mother's womb. Not one day has slipped by without Him being there; in the sweat, tears, blood and laughter. Calling your name and wooing your heart.

But we are so afraid. We're reluctant to share them for fear of how our stories might be heard, and handled. Balked at. Or even dismissed.

The heart ache we've experienced might pale in comparison to someone else's tale of agony. So we leave it on the shelf.

The mistakes we've made stir up the shame we've mastered the art of silencing. Only to discover it cannot and will not be silenced. It creates a low, nauseating hum that permeates everything we do. We feel its vibration in every area of our lives.

The particularly dark chapters are uncomfortable to revisit, not to mention terrifying to divulge, so we stuff them down into the crevices of our souls for safe-keeping.

We hold our stories close to our chests, protective of the narrative within. Unsure of whether our hearts can handle the exposure.

When a crack of light beckons us to come, bring our heavy burdens, and bear our souls, the questions pummel us back into silence.

...What if I lose their love? Their respect? Their trust? Heck, what if I lose everything?

...What if what I share confirms what I already know about myself...I am unlovely and unwanted?

...What if I'm shunned? Rejected? Humiliated and finally excluded?

...What if they pity me? Judge me?

...And use the lens from my broken past to make assumptions about my future?

We worry people will wrap us today in the flesh of our past, and then superimpose their assumed outcome over our lives tomorrow?

As the fear consumes us, we wonder...wouldn't it just be better to keep our story safely tucked away on pages between dusty covers in the recesses of our closets? We assume silence keeps us safe, but we've bought into an illusion.

> Stories kept in secret, stashed away in dark corners, fester and take on a life of their own. They hold us on a short leash, whispering warnings of rejection if the word gets out, and offer us a place to hide.

And herein lies the problem; hiding.

Adam and Eve[11] got the ball rolling when they sought refuge among the trees of the garden after eating the forbidden fruit, and we've been hiding ever since. The very first humans were driven there by the very same things that keep us there today: fear and shame.

Shame manages to convince us that who we are is not enough. Our brokenness renders us unworthy and telling our story would simply confirm it. So a mask and an accompanying masquerade are in order to make us more acceptable.

But it's a lie. One that manages to keep us silent and suffering in isolation when freedom and power are but an arm's-length away. I believed the lie for too long and the weight of carrying it alone nearly destroyed me. I wove tall tales of accomplishment and prestige that served as a fairly believable mask for years. But rather than provide relief, it drove me further into hiding. The web of lies held me hostage for several years before I mustered the courage to climb out.

The pain of exposure finally seemed less painful than allowing my soul to continue imploding.

You see, those stories we stuff down - the ones too colorful and obscure to be believed, or maybe too dark and weighty to be read aloud - those stories need to be shared too. Not recklessly with the masses - for not everyone knows how to handle our story - but with a select few. And then, as shame loosens its grip, with more people and with more volume.

And then maybe someday, when you find your story no longer has any power over you, but rather through you it serves to encourage and empower others, possibly even from a platform.

Because, Jehovah Sneaky. 'Nuff said.

When I finally tip-toed into the light, two months before getting married, it changed my life. And what amazes me still is that the very things that seemed to threaten to destroy me have become the very same things that connect my heart to others, compelling and shaping the heart of my ministry. My broken story, redeemed.

The incredible thing about stories is the way our brains process them. We may not remember the details shared, or even the bottom-line of the story, but we always remember the emotions they stirred in us and the way they moved us. This is because stories bypass the hard logic centers of the brain and move the tender, nostalgic places of the heart. This explains why Jesus always taught in parables and why the best teachers still pepper their talks with them. And it's why telling my story, over a decade later, still wrecks me in the most beautiful of ways.

"Our deepest fear is not that we are inadequate. Our deepest fear is that we are powerful beyond measure. It is our light, not our darkness that most frightens us. We ask ourselves, who am I to be brilliant, gorgeous, talented, fabulous? Actually, who are you not to be?

You are a child of God. Your playing small does not serve the world. There is nothing enlightened about shrinking so that other people won't feel insecure around you. We are all meant to shine, as children do. We were born to make manifest the glory of God that is

within us. It's not just in some of us; it's in everyone. And
as we let our own light shine, we unconsciously give
other people permission to do the same. As we are
liberated from our own fear, our presence
automatically liberates others."
Marianne Williamson

COFFEE & THERMOSTATS

While you've no doubt heard the old tale of the mother who
wanted to teach her daughter a powerful object lesson with
three simple ingredients, it bears repeating.

While the adult daughter pours out her heart to her mom,
the wise mother leads her to the kitchen where she puts three
pots of water on the stove. Once the water starts to boil, the
mother puts a handful of carrots in the first pot, an egg in the
next, and some ground coffee beans in the last. After twenty
minutes of listening to her daughter describe how hard her life
is and how she's not sure she can handle much more, the
mother quietly scoops the carrots and egg out into bowls,
pouring the contents of the third pot into another bowl.

"Tell me, what do you see, honey?", she asks her visibly
perplexed daughter.

"Well, carrots, an egg and...some coffee?", she answers.

Inviting her daughter to feel the carrots, she notes that
they're soft. "What about the egg?", she asks, encouraging
her to break it. Removing the shell, she finds what she
expected, a hard-boiled egg. Finally, the mother offers the
small bowl of coffee. Sipping it, the daughter closes her eyes
and smiles.

"So, mom", the daughter inquires, "what's this all about?"

Her mother explains that each of the objects experienced
the same adversity - boiling water - but that each reacted

differently. The carrots went in strong, hard and unrelenting, but emerged soft and weak. The egg had been fragile, its outer shell protecting its fluid interior. But after being jostled in the boiling water, its insides became hardened.

The ground coffee beans had behaved uniquely, however. While the first two had been changed by their surroundings, the beans had actually changed the water.

"Which one will you be?" she asked her daughter. "When adversity surrounds you, how will you respond...like the carrots, the egg, or the coffee beans?"

While I've heard this story over a dozen times, and tend to mentally fill in the blanks and poo-poo it when it gets shared, the lessons it teaches are timeless and are worth soaking in for just a while. Reread it if you blew through it, would you? It's profound.

It begs the question: which one have I been in the story of my life? And which one will I choose to be from here on out?

...The carrots that seem strong and tough, but in the face of pain, when adversity arises, I wilt and lose my strength.
...The egg that started with a malleable heart and a fluid spirit, but through the trials of life became hard and stiff. Has your tough shell remained intact, but beneath it you carry a hardened heart and stiff spirit?
...Or are we like the coffee bean that, through the heat of life, releases its fragrance and flavor and transforms its environment?

Eleanor Roosevelt expressed the same sentiment, only with a different hot beverage with her famous quote, "a woman is like a tea bag - you never know how strong she is until she gets in hot water".

> You and I were created to be thermostats, not thermometers. Thermometers simply register and read the temperature around them, while thermostats determine it. And then work to maintain it.

They are not helpless victims of their circumstance, they are powerful influencers and changers of them. We were born to be agents of change, not casualties of life.

Many, if not all, of the people I admire and respect as leaders and pioneers have become the people they are, with the ability to speak into others' lives and impact the world, because of the hell they've been through. Because of heart-ache, devastation, gut-wrenching loss, disability, bankruptcy, or disaster, these people have risen from the ashes with a tenacity, resilience and heart to do what really matters. Not in spite of pain and discomfort, but because of it. And their stories move us and wake us.

We all experience pain, we all walk through loss of some kind. We all struggle. But it's what we do with the broken pieces of the mosaic that matters. The world will chew us up and spit us out, but then we get to decide what we're going to do next. Will we pick up the shattered fragments and allow God to create a masterpiece out of our messes, or will we throw them in a box and hide it in the basement so others won't see our chipped paint and jagged edges?

I've got news for you, sister. It's those very things that wounded you, and that you now hide, that will become your platform for impact - if you allow them to. Those things I kept in secret for so long, that I dragged around like thousand pound weights around my neck for 7 years. They have become my favorite stories to share because they speak of a love so radical and a redemption so complete that I cannot keep them to myself. I simply cannot.

What we tend to forget in the midst of our story-stuffing, demon-taming and mask-wearing is this: our story isn't for us in the first place. It never was. It's for others, and those others need you to own it and share it. Your story isn't just a past to regret and resent and hide, it's a brush stroke on a massive canvas that reveals a greater story. As you take your nose from that dark spot you've been pressed up against, and step back, you'll start to see the bigger picture taking shape.

My past no longer defines me, but it has shaped me into who I am today. What once terrified me now compels me. To love, serve, encourage and equip others who are gasping for life beneath the crippling weight of shame.

You need to know; it won't be easy. In fact it may be excruciating for a season as you willingly step into those dark places and sink your fingers into the dirt. But believe me when I say...the temporary pain of unpacking your baggage and learning to travel lightly isn't nearly as emotionally exhausting as spending the rest of your life trying to keep the dirt hidden. Running from our past will always be more destructive than facing it and leaning into it.

"Owning our story and loving ourselves through that process is the bravest thing that we will ever do."
Brené Brown

WHAT'S YOUR STORY?

In every great story there is both beauty and heartache. Woven into every plotline is success and struggle. No story worth telling exists without both triumph and tragedy, and a point in which the protagonist must decide what he or she will do with the latter. In fact, you are not an overcomer until you've had something to overcome. The hero and the coward face the very same thing; it is how they respond to their struggle that sets them apart. This is the turning point that makes or breaks the story.

What is your story, and what will you do with it?

Get yourself prayed up, muster every ounce of courage you've got, and go unpack those bags you've been dragging around. Gather one or two close friends who can be available to help you pick up the pieces and remove the shrapnel when needed. Choose to stop fighting the pain and allow yourself to sit with it. Feel all the feelings you've been avoiding, just for a moment, cry your brains out if necessary, and then let those feelings go. The process of extracting the treasure from the dirt will be a messy one, but it will always, always be a worthwhile one.

You have a story, beloved and it's a story we need to hear...because yours is a part of mine, and mine is a part of yours, and together we make up a greater tale of messy humanity and faithful redemption, of strength in weakness and beauty in brokenness.

The beautiful thing about owning your story is that it empowers you to help write the ending.

It's your story, live a good one.

> *"There is no greater agony than bearing an untold story inside you."*
> Maya Angelou

DIG DEEPER ON PAGE 22
OF THE STUDY GUIDE

CHAPTER 7

N | NEVER EVER GIVE UP

"Never give up on a dream
just because of the time it will
take to accomplish it.
The time will pass anyway."

EARL NIGHTINGALE

When you move across the world three times as a teenager, attending four different high schools along the way, it's probably not unusual to feel a little confused about life.

When the time came to start planning and doing college prep, I felt lost. After all, these kids had been having this conversation since their sophomore year, and I showed up in time to start our senior year from a school system across the pond that did things very differently. Not to mention the fact that it was an Afrikaans school. I'm quite sure I missed half of what was said there that year.

While these kids were submitting college applications, visiting campuses, and talking majors and minors, I was quite certain they were speaking another language. I didn't have a clue where I wanted to go, what I wanted to study, or even what I wanted to be when I grew up.

I'd always loved a myriad of things, from art class and choir, to biology and history, but never felt a distinct draw in one direction or another. Besides, I couldn't make a living being a mermaid or a trapeze artist, so I was going to have to compromise right off the bat.

Reading books and writing papers felt daunting, math was overwhelming, and I'd like to avoid the subject of chemistry altogether.

While I didn't know what I wanted, I could tell you what I didn't want. I didn't want to punch the clock at a job I loathed, or sit in a cubicle and allow my soul to get sucked dry while padding my 401K. I didn't want to be a doctor because blood still makes me pass out, I didn't want to be a teacher (mostly because both my parents were teachers and there may have been some rebellion going on), and I didn't want to show up day after day to help make someone else's dream a reality.

I liked the image of the woman in business. She always looked so confident and put together in those stock images, what with her Starbucks coffee in one hand, briefcase in the other, rocking her classic black heels. The quintessential 'strong, confident female'. And yet the business world terrified me. If I didn't have the guts to try out for the school play, how on earth would I survive in the corporate world?

So I signed up for the Massage Therapy certification program at the local community college, go figure, and called it a day. My passion for the subject spread about as far as the anatomy lab and physiology classes and stopped just short of the naked people on tables that I was supposed to rub down for an hour. I endured the two years only to finish what I had started, and then walked away, never looking back.

While rubbing shoulders with the holistic crowd at college, I got sucked into the fitness world. I started taking fitness instructor classes and eventually signed up for a personal trainer course. At least something good came out of my college classes, I figured.

To help pay for college I started working at Pier 1 Imports right out of high school, moving to the restaurant world for a brief stint, and eventually into Christian radio. It was here that I started to dabble in, and fall in love with, voice work and public speaking. I started leading small groups through church and had discovered a real love for teaching (don't tell my parents), and suddenly had a larger platform from which to share. I also started to tinker in layout and graphics as a way to remedy the severe case of heinous documents and newsletter design they were experiencing.

I left the radio station after a few years to help launch a women's gym, where I discovered a love for wordsmithing marketing material and brand development (not that I knew at the time what either of those things were). I loved the creative freedom I had, but soon discovered the weight of a brick-and-mortar business was not one I ever wanted to shoulder.

Now 24 and married, I still had no idea what I wanted to do with my life. I could not for the life of me pin point one thing I wanted to do when I grew up, and it distressed me. What was wrong with me? Why couldn't I just name something and go after it like everyone else?

Oh, how desperately I wish I could step back in time and whisper in my own ear, "it's not because you're broken or lazy or lack ambition...it's because you're finding your way to something gloriously unique and there is no shortcut. Keep putting one foot in front of the other. This wild and winding path is the exact one you're supposed to be on. Keep dabbling and searching and dreaming and playing and risking and failing...you're right on schedule".

"Don't tell me the sky's the limit when there are footprints on the moon."
Paul Brandt

I dabbled in a couple of direct-marketing businesses in an effort to work from home and make money, but found the pressure to recruit team-members, sell products and hit monthly targets caused an anxiety I couldn't wait to shake. The only things I wanted to sell, if I had to peddle wares at all, were my own creations - whatever those might be.

I moved on to another gym where I worked as their marketing director and a personal trainer until the 39th week of my first pregnancy. I went back for a few weeks after maternity leave and just couldn't do it. My indifference had turned to an intense dislike for my job. Despite their best efforts to accommodate my schedule by letting me take my daughter to work with me on occasion, I just couldn't' do work I didn't love while trying to navigate the new waters of motherhood.

I pleaded with God to give me something I could do from home that would satisfy the deep ache in my soul to do creative work that mattered, while affording me the flexibility to focus on my family first.

I had started blogging my motherhood journey in an effort to keep our overseas family in the loop and to, let's be honest, not go insane in the process of mothering a tiny human. Loving the reach of an online platform, I started sharing designs I'd created for family and friends in, wait for it....Microsoft Publisher. I was approached by a friend of a friend who was getting married and needed wedding invitations, programs and a seating chart. I didn't have a clue what I was doing, but I took it as a gift from God and set about Googling, "what is a seating chart?". I found myself a friendly local printer and started exploring paper, pixels and pantone colors.

Without a single business bone in my body, and without any formal training in the field, I started my little graphic design business. I eventually upgraded from Publisher to Photoshop Elements, and dropped the .blogger in my .com in favor of a custom domain name, and continued to not have a clue what I was doing, but loved every minute of the discovery.

It was 2007, and for the first time in my adult life, I was doing something that truly lit my heart on fire. As it turns out, all the symptoms I'd been experiencing growing up without a clear cut idea of what I wanted, but with a distinct understanding of what I didn't want, pointed straight to the wonderful world of the creative entrepreneur.

I continued to write my heart out on the blog, hashing out my thoughts on everything from motherhood and marriage to gardening and spirituality. I loved the creative freedom I had to dabble in different things; sharing recipes, DIY craft projects, and designs I had turned into free printables, all the while documenting life through my new love of photography.

Over time, and through many ridiculous name changes, I expanded my blog into a business to cover my growing speaking ministry and new found passion for designing things with swirls and stripes. When the idea to have a merchandise table at my events popped up, I was giddy. Suddenly I had an avenue to sell random products I was feeling the itch to create, without having to manage an online store and keep items in stock.

Then came my passion for coaching, which helped give birth to my first book, and my little business grew. I eventually added consulting under the coaching umbrella, and launched an online branch of the shop.

Of all the things I get to do through Simply Bloom today, speaking may be my absolute favorite. I love everything about it; the prayerful preparation and research that goes into each message, the high-energy performance component of delivering a talk, the dopamine that surges as I walk off a stage, and the mind-blowingly beautiful conversations I get to have with people afterwards. This right here is the cherry on top of an already delicious dessert.

"It's never too late to be who you might have been"
George Elliot

STUMBLING OUR WAY INTO DESTINY

With my entrepreneurial fingers now stuck in several pies, I have to wonder...had I known that this was even an option, how would I have wrapped it all up into a concise response to that famous question, "what do you want to be when you grow up?"

This. Exactly this. *All* of this.

But here's the thing; how would I have known had I not stepped out and experimented. Dabbled, risked appearing flakey, experimented, tried things I failed miserably at, and discovered things that made my spirit leap. I've launched things that months later have made me want to cry, thinking "what the heck was I thinking?! I don't want to do this!". I'm learning that it's not just about possibility, it's also very much about pleasure. I don't want to just do what's possible, I want to accomplish things that bring life and joy.

My dream job wasn't in a text book somewhere. What I do - and love - cannot be neatly labeled and put in a box. Because it's fluid and alive and evolving all the time.

"Miracles start to happen when you give as much energy to your dreams as you do to your fears."
Richard Wilkins

I'm right where I need to be today. And five years ago, 10,000 steps back, I was exactly where I needed to be then. And I'm going to keep putting one foot in front of the other so in five more years, I'll be right where I need to be there.

The truth is, I have stumbled my way into almost everything I do today. From the community we live in and love on, to the items I design and sell in my shop. From the couples we mentor (and the mere fact that I actually get to mentor people) to the platforms I get to speak on. I could never have predicted this life. And had I tried, it would have been a dull, monochromatic reflection of what it is today.

I may be passionate and driven and fiercely goal oriented today, but to be honest, I'm not sure there's a single straight line on the map of my life, bar the red thread of grace.

And while this chapter may feel like one rambling story, what I want you to hear is this; keep trying, keep showing up, keep experimenting, keep discovering. Don't be afraid to lay things down. But don't ever, ever give up.

While I've heard it quoted in many different ways, I love how Thomas Edison is recorded as having declared that he didn't fail, in regards to his inventing of the electric light bulb, he simply found 10,000 ways that didn't work. Had he given up after the first attempt, or even the hundredth, how different our lives would be.

Had the Israelites stopped marching around Jericho on the 6th time around because not a single stone was falling and because trumpets were not their weapon of choice, how differently that story would have ended.

NOT WRONG, JUST DIFFERENT

Every creative endeavor you set out on, whether it becomes a part of your repertoire or not, is a breadcrumb on your journey. It's all a part of finding out who you are on this journey to uncovering and igniting your passion. It's not a destination you arrive at. And it never will be. You can travel west until the cows come home and you'll never arrive at a place called "West".

It is quite simply the fuel that propels and compels us in the direction of our calling. Together with our purpose, it is what keeps our minds buzzing at night, and what gets us moving in the morning. While we do get a clearer, more defined sense of the things we're passionate about as we press into them and handle them, we cannot neatly package up our passion, slap a bow on it or even file it in a compartment.

Passion can be defined, but it will not be confined. It is effervescent and alive, moving and dancing and growing as we do.

One step forward, two steps back, one to the side, now turn around. And yes, occasionally there's a "we all fall down" move. But don't worry, it's always followed by the "get back up" maneuver.

*"Always be a first-rate version of yourself
instead of a second-rate version of someone else"*
Judy Garland

It's easy to feel like a failure when you've fluttered from one thing to another in an effort to figure out where your soul ignites; in search of your "thing". But I'm learning that we don't have to have just one thing. Emilie Wapnick calls this eclectic Jane-of-all-trades a Multipotentialite[12]. I thrive off having multiple areas of passion and expertise, and the areas where they overlap are my sweet spot. I would never have found them had I not been willing to look foolish and blaze my own trail. I haven't yet discovered all the things I'm passionate about, but I have found plenty that I'm not. And I wouldn't have figured this out had I not stuck my finger in the pie and given it a try. Maybe you can relate?

Don't ever stop trying, dabbling, refining. Practice your passions and learn to play with your dreams. It isn't about perfection (when is it, really?), it's all about discovery. A river doesn't cut through rock because of its incredible power and precision, but because of its unrelenting presence and persistence.

There is no manual for the passionate life. It's a wild adventure of taking one brave step after another, taking your creative pulse, keeping your ear tuned to the heavens, and moving forward.

It doesn't matter what people think. If you've got entrepreneurial blood in your veins, you're a different breed of business person and you won't be understood by people who love their nine to fiver. And the Lord knows we need them. If it gives you life to write legacy on the young lives in your home, while creating exquisite meals and glitter-encrusted art projects, throw yourself into it. We need passionate people in every field; from janitors to baristas, from CPAs to SAHMs.

Repeat after me, "it's not wrong, it's just different".

.

Whatever it is that lights your fire - find it and feed it - because it wakes up your soul and we need your soul fully awake.

And When the little voice in your head - which sounds strangely like your own - says, "It's time to give this up", choose rather to listen to the voice of hope that says, "Let's give it one more shot...we got this!".

"Hold fast to dreams for if dreams die,
Life is a broken-winged bird that cannot fly."
Langston Hughes.

DIG DEEPER ON PAGE 24
OF THE STUDY GUIDE

In the next section we'll be taking what we've learned about our PASSION and will fold it into our PURPOSE. Hold on to your hat because when these two get together, wildly beautiful things start to happen.

"If you can't figure out your purpose, figure out your passion. For your passion will lead you right to your purpose"

BISHOP T.D. JAKES

PURPOSE

"The place God calls you to is the place where your deep gladness and the world's deep hunger meet"

FREDERICK BUECHNER

The small group of female entrepreneurs that I meet with weekly gathered to hear the heart behind a new organization to be launched in the Fall. With my two little ones freshly out of school for the summer, and the warm sun begging us to emerge from inside, we packed lunches and gathered at the park.

As Alathea and Aiden ran and shrieked and climbed, she shared jaw-dropping statistics about the startling number of homeless families in our community, and the even more crushing number of young women who have become victims of human trafficking in our area.

Story after story, statistic after statistic.

As if cued by the weight of the topic, clouds rolled in and the heavens broke open. Seeking refuge beneath a nearby pavilion from the sudden downpour, we asked questions, made connections and offered suggestions.

I was amazed by a common thread that emerged in both the issue of homelessness and human trafficking. A lack of identity and purpose were prevalent in both people groups.

The men and women caught in the generational cycle of unemployment-by-choice, content to live off 'the system' and raise their families on welfare, and those young women preyed on and lured away by predators, both lived with a severe lack of self-value and purpose.

In the same way a young man can learn to silence the ache for adventure and reward-driven labor by losing sight of why he's uniquely created to accomplish something extraordinary in this world, a young woman can lose sight of her value and fall prey to the insidious tentacles of trafficking.

While it may seem like an odd connection to make, purpose and identity do go hand in hand, as do a lack of purpose and the loss of true identity.

It's simply impossible to develop the one without tapping into the other, or to lose one without crippling the other. They are intricately connected and always interdependent.

Purpose is a wildly popular topic. There are 61,629 books in Amazon alone on the topic. Everyone seems to be hunting for this elusive golden ticket to living fully alive. But purpose isn't something you wake up and discover all of a sudden. Or a place you arrive at. It is so much more about *destiny*, than *destination*.

Rather than the red-starred endpoint we arrive at on a map after a 23 hour road trip, it's the way in which we get there. It's the direction in which we travel, and the discovery of new facets along the winding, detour-filled way.

It's the reason we travel in the first place.

Passion is fabulous - and essential to the journey - but without a *need* to be met, our passion lacks purpose. True success in life comes when you make an impact on others, not just a good life for yourself.

And this is where purpose comes in.

In this segment we'll unpack what it means to step into our calling. We'll explore how critical our definitions of success and failure are to our ability to step out of our comfort zones, and how the positioning of ourselves as conduits helps graft us into something far greater and more beautiful than we could have accomplished on our own.

Let's do this!

"Tell me, what is it you plan to do with
your one wild and precious life?"
Mary Oliver

CHAPTER 8

P | POWER UP YOUR STRENGTHS

"Everybody is a genius.
But if you judge a fish by
its ability to climb a tree,
it will live its whole life
believing that it is stupid"

ALBERT EINSTEIN

There's a story told about Margaret Thatcher, towards the end of her tenure as the Prime Minister of the United Kingdom, while she was visiting a retirement home in the country. Moving from room to room, she sat and chatted with the residents. She was talking to one particular older woman when she realized that there wasn't an inkling of recognition on the woman's face. She seemed to have no idea that she was in fact speaking with the "Iron Lady".

"Do you know who I am?", Margaret asked her. "No, dear, but if you ask the nurse, she can remind you".

Do you know who you are? It's not uncommon for people to respond to that question with a list of the many hats they wear, roles they play and titles they've earned.

But that's not what I'm asking. Who are you...really, really?

Not what do you do, or how does your email footer describe you, or what does your name tag say, but who are you? And how did you get that way?". This is the question I love to ask people I'm just getting to know, hopefully over an extra hot soy latte. In other words, what's your story and have you owned it yet?

Who are you? Do you know?

If I dig deeply and really press into the women I meet, many will sigh and respond with mild distress and a deflated spirit, "I don't even know any more". This is an especially common response for young moms who've thrown themselves into keeping little humans alive, only to lose themselves in the process.

Because you're this far into this book - and are reading a book like this in the first place - I'm assuming you have an inkling of who you are or you're on the journey to finding out. Maybe you're keenly aware of the fire in your bones (even if you're not sure what it is), and you're beginning to tune into that inner voice that reminds you that you were created for more than this.

The exciting thing about the way we're made is that the things we're naturally good at and the things we're passionate about often point to our purpose. Maybe not directly, but they are brilliantly interconnected.

I realize we dug into this in the Passion segment, but in the light of Purpose, let me ask you again, "what do you love to do?". And I'm talking about a 'tickles your toes, delights your soul, emerges effortlessly from you' kind of love? Take a moment to think about it.

Your answer is a natural segue into the next question, "what are you good at?".

It saddens me that while we talk easily about what we're excited about, and can rattle off numerous things we're not good at, many of us struggle to point out things we are really good at.

Some adhere to the thinking that it's prideful to focus on one's strengths or get too well acquainted with the things one excels at. Others may have been taught that true humility doesn't answer that question confidently, with a list of things one's good at. Rather it shuffles awkwardly, toeing the carpet, shyly delivering a half-baked response followed by a quick gush of inadequacies.

Maybe you've bought into the lie that the best way to be useful in this world is to stop messing around with your strengths and focus rather on all those things you stink at. Those are what've been tripping you up. You've got to get good at all those things you're not good at first. Then, and only then, will your life have influence and impact.

If that's you, you've been sold a bill of goods and we're about to return that bad boy to the store.

"Success is achieved by developing our strengths, not by eliminating our weaknesses."
Marilyn vos Savant

THE BEAUTY OF WEAKNESS

Before we unwrap the power of strengths, I want to tackle the subject of weakness (because the struggle is real).

While I spent many of my younger years hiding, resenting or attempting to correct my areas of weakness, I am learning to embrace them. In part because they're exhausting to manage and it leaves me feeling defeated and frustrated. But mostly for two central - and maybe surprising - reasons:

• Because our weakness drives us into community. We need each other, in fact we were made with each other in mind. For example; while you're excellent at doing A, you struggle with B. But B is my favorite thing to do! This gal we both know is brilliant with C, which is my least favorite thing to do (and I truly stink at it), but she needs help with A. Which is totally *your* thing. As we do life together, sharing our strengths and weaknesses with each other, we create a beautiful picture of the human body functioning healthily with all its active parts doing their thing for the health of the whole. Weakness puts the beauty of community on display.

On a purely practical note, if you run an organization or business, it's incredibly wise to outsource your weaknesses. This way you're free to spend most of your time and energy finding the sweet spot between what you love and what you're good at. Find people whose area of strength covers your area of weakness and enlist their help.

• Because our weakness is where we get to see God extravagantly come through for us. As Paul writes in 2 Corinthians 12:9[13], we experience God's strength and grace in the midst of our weakness, and if embracing those offerings means also embracing my weakness, I'm in.

Yes, it's important to know where your areas of weakness are - in fact it's liberating to acknowledge them - but it's unproductive to dwell on them. One of the reasons people struggle to answer the question, "what are you good at?" but are quick to answer "but I'm not good at..." is because of the misconception that by focusing on and micromanaging our weaknesses, we'll do less damage.

Contrary to popular belief, we don't do the most damage in our areas of weakness, we wreak the most havoc by misappropriating our strengths.

Read that again. It's profound.

This concept blew my mind when I first heard it during a StrengthsFinder[14] class. And while it may seem an odd observation, it makes perfect sense. Just think of Hitler and Stalin. They were charismatic leaders and gifted communicators who had the ability to ignite and activate their followers, and they used their strengths for the destruction and dishonoring of human life.

IT'S YOUR PARTY, GET UNWRAPPED

You were woven together in your mother's womb for such a time as this, with all those quirks and inclinations that make up your personality and style. You had hardwired into you before the foundation of the earth a unique cluster of giftings, a purpose to flesh out, and a distinct set of strengths and skills that you'll spend your life honing.

The sooner you start unwrapping those gifts, exploring your strengths and enjoying the way God made you, the more authentically impactful your influence will be on the lives around you.

With that in mind, I want to invite you to get excited about your strengths. If you're a 'rule follower', consider this your permission slip to enjoy the process of discovering how you're uniquely wired and who you're truly knit together to be. The journey is half the fun.

I love what Sally Hogshead says with regard to uncovering your distinct expression; "different is better than better". Amen, sister! Sure, we can work tirelessly to be the best at something, but there'll always be someone better, and then we'll just have to work harder. What if we took that energy and funneled it into figuring out what makes us, well...US. Can you imagine how the world would change if we stopped trying to be like other people and learned how to be the best version of ourselves?

Just embracing the fact that we can be uniquely excellent at something - in being different - sets us apart from the herd.

> *"It takes courage to grow up and*
> *become who you really are."*
> *E.E. Cummings*

As I've explored the world of coaching and mentoring over the past few years, the more I've realized that this basic level of self-discovery is a crucial piece of the purpose puzzle. Discovering your unique personality, temperament, gifts, strengths and love languages - and the stunning way they work together to make you who you are - is an excellent way to get to know yourself and intentionally take strides in pursuing what it is that sets your soul on fire. After all, how do we move ahead when we don't understand the 'vehicle' in which we travel, or the method and style of that movement?

I have a confession to make; I'm somewhat of a self-awareness junkie. Taking tests and assessments is my jam. If I hear about a new one that reveals a different aspect of one's personality or leadership style, I'm on it like white on rice. While tests are not without error, and shouldn't be regarded as gospel truth, they offer insight into the way we see the world, process information and make decisions, and in doing so, they help us become more mindful and effective in our mission.

Below is a list of online tests that are·not only fun, but enlightening and revelatory. Most are free.

There's nothing quite like reading results with a resounding..."yes! That's totally me! Who knew I wasn't the only one who processed life this way" or "no wonder I tend to respond to conflict that way!" or "why of course I gravitate towards that...it's because I'm wired like this!"

Please note that these 'tests' are not intended to be labels, nor are they attempts to shove you into a neat little category or box. No man-made assessment has the capability to figure us out completely. We are far too complex and multi-dimensional for that. They offer but a piece of the puzzle, together painting a pretty good picture of why we think and behave the way we do, and that's a great place to start on our journey to awakening your purpose.

PERSONALITY TESTS:

• **16 Personalities*** : https://www.16personalities.com/free-personality-test

• **HumanMetrics*** : http://www.humanmetrics.com/cgi-win/jtypes2.asp

• **Memorado*** : https://memorado.com/pti_test

• **Personality Pathways*** :
http://www.personalitypathways.com/type_inventory.html

  (very brief, but has a great overview of the E/I, S/N, T/F & J/P)

• **Celebrity Types*** :
http://www.celebritytypes.com/personality-tests.php

(This one offers a lot of other silliness mixed in with personality test)

*These personality tests above are based on the Myers-Briggs style assessment, some more professionally than others.

Carl Jung, a renowned Swiss psychiatrist, characterized people using three criteria:

• E or I (Extroversion or Introversion) | Where, primarily, do you prefer to direct your energy?

• S or N (Sensing or iNtuition) | How do you prefer to process information?

• J or P (Judgment or Perception) | How do you prefer to organize your life?

The mother-daughter team, Katharine Cook Briggs and Isabel Briggs Myers, took Jung's extensive research and, by adding a fourth criterion, developed a questionnaire.

• T or F (Thinking or Feeling) | How do you prefer to make decisions?

This assessment results in the 16 personality/temperament types. You may find that you get slightly different results from the different tests. Sometimes that's due to not fully understanding the question or answering from what you desire versus what you actually do. I have found that taking a few over the course of a few days allows me to get a handle on the different types, narrow down the results, and really hammer out my 'type'.

- 41 Questions, 1 Personality : www.41q.com/

- **Personality Plus** : www.41q.com/ (this is a PDF download)

STRENGTHS

- **Strengths Test** : www.freestrengthstest.workuno.com/free-strengths-test.html

- **Strengths & Weaknesses Aptitude Test** : www.richardstep.com/richardstep-strengths-weaknesses-aptitude-test

- **StrengthsFinder** : www.strengths.gallup.com/110440/About-StrengthsFinder-20.aspx

(this 'Top 5' version costs around $15, and serves as a great introduction to the official StrengthsFinder material. If it's at all possible for you to take a class/course, I would highly recommend it as you'll be able to dig into the meat of this incredible research and explore the ins and outs of your top 5 as they pertain to your roles, and as they relate to those of your team, ministry, or spouses', etc.)

OTHER TESTS & ASSESSMENTS:

- **5 Love Languages** : www.5lovelanguages.com/profile/ (excellent for marriages, parentings, business relationships and friendships)

- **Emotional I.Q.** : www.ihhp.com/free-eq-quiz/

- **The Fascination Advantage** : www.howtheworldseesyou.com/fascination-advantage-assessment/

SPIRITUAL DEVELOPMENT:

- **Spiritual Gifts Test** : www.spiritualgiftstest.com/test/adult

- **Gifts Test** : www.giftstest.com

- **The 3 Colors of Ministry** :
www.3colorworld.org/en/etests/ministry/summary/about

(this requires setting up an account and a small fee, but it is incredibly insightful when it comes to identifying and developing your unique spiritual gifts)

- **S.H.A.P.E.*** : http://www.sdfa.org/pdf/shape-test.pdf (one of several free assessments available online)

---

*S.H.A.P.E. comes out of Saddleback[15] and is designed to explore the 'Five Ways God Has Shaped You', tapping into other already existing analysis like spiritual gifts and personality profiles:

S | Spiritual Gifts : What has God supernaturally gifted me to do?

H | Heart : What do I have passion for and love to do?

A | Abilities : What natural talents and skills do I have?

P | Personality : Where does my personality best suit me to serve?

E | Experiences : What spiritual experiences have I had? What painful experiences have I had? What educational experiences have I had? What ministry experiences have I had?

"Hide not your talents. They for use were made.
What's a sundial in the shade?"
Benjamin Franklin

Once you've taken a couple of tests, you'll start to see evidence of the results playing out in everyday life. You'll identify trends in the way you process situations, how you respond to people and things, and the way in which you naturally flesh out your default settings.

DIFFERENCES & MARRIAGE

My husband and I often take tests together (or I manage to convince him he needs to take yet another one I've found), and our results are always really revealing. While our core values and foundational beliefs are the same, we are complete opposites in most areas.

I am an ENFP girl, while he is an ISTJ guy.

When it comes to the 5 Love Languages, I'm a 'words of affirmation' and 'acts of 'service' girl (with a side of 'gifts'), while his main love languages are 'quality time' and 'physical touch'. Go figure.

Our StrengthFinders results are profoundly insightful as well. One of my top 5 strengths is 'positivity', which explains my need to carefully filter what media I consume - news and negativity have a crippling effect on me and literally make me feel like my soul is suffocating. One of my hubby's top strengths, 'context', help him do his job really well - as an officer, processing negativity and using it to carefully evaluate his surroundings helps keep him alive.

Not only did taking these tests together give each of us a fresh appreciation for how the other is wired, but it helps us not get caught up in banging heads over things that don't really matter. I no longer try to get him to think like me, and he no longer expects me to see the world through his lens. Rather than argue over why we see the world so differently, we're now free to celebrate how uniquely God has made each of us, and how much we need those qualities found in each other.

My husband is the rock to my balloon. Another balloon wouldn't secure me, I desperately need all he brings to the table. I love the way he grounds me with his practical perspective, rock-solid wisdom and contextual insight. And he doesn't need another rock, especially in his line of work. He desperately needs the hope, positivity and playfulness I bring to the table to counteract the heaviness he wades through.

When it comes to expressing love, we are forced to step outside of ourselves and become fluent in each other's 'languages' if we want to express them in a way that the other receives them best. A greater level of intentionality and selflessness is always beneficial to marriage.

While it takes work and requires bucket-loads of grace, we need each other to be fully who we were made to be, not a sub-standard, resentful imitation of ourselves. Remember our motto, "it's not wrong, it's just different"? It really comes in handy here.

You'll discover that knowing you're different – and that you were made that way on purpose – actually helps keep the peace and helps add weight and value to why you both think and behave the way you do. It's incredibly liberating to acknowledge and embrace your differences rather than resent them and attempt to change one another.

So as it turns out, opposites do in fact attract!

DIFFERENCES & PARENTING

I remember hearing an interesting take on Proverbs 22:6 some time ago during a Podcast that I cannot seem to track down. While I hesitate to share something I cannot credit, it really struck me and I feel the insight is worth sharing.

> *"Start children off on the way they should go, and even when they are old they will not turn from it."*
> Proverbs 22:6

This proverb is almost always associated with discipline and spiritual direction, but the podcaster mentioned that the root of the word, in the original text, may have more accurately been translated as 'bent'; as in 'bring up a child in the way they are bent'. This speaks to our incredible ability, as parents, to raise our children to be sensitive to who they are and what they're drawn to (and I'm not referring to childish folly or sin).

What if we taught our kids at a young age to listen to and explore their gifts and talents, and to flourish in the areas they naturally excel? If spending our lives exhaling what God breathed into us is one of our greatest responsibilities, would this not be a worthy interpretation of this scripture? Wouldn't it be better to equip them to succeed at being the best version of themselves, how God made them, than bend them in the way we feel, or society says, they should go?

> *"Children aren't things to be molded,*
> *but people to be unfolded"*
> Jess Lair

What is the common thread that has run through their hobbies over the years? What are they naturally good at?

What are they drawn to? What devastates them? How do they naturally express themselves? How they show their love for you is a powerful indicator of how they need your love expressed toward them (refer to the 5 Love Languages).

These are all questions we need to be asking if we want to help our children blossom into the young men and women they're called to be. I want to do everything I can as a parent to help my children flesh out the unique plan God has for them, and by teaching them to tune into their own passion and purpose we can help propel them into the future they were created for.

"Your ministry will be most effective and fulfilling when you are using your gifts and abilities in the area of your heart's desire in a way that best expresses your personality and experience."
Rick Warren

DIG DEEPER ON PAGE 29
OF THE STUDY GUIDE

CHAPTER 9

U | UNEARTH THE PICTURE

"The two most important days in
your life are the day you are born
and the day you find out why."

MARK TWAIN

Dan Miller [16]tells the story of an old rabbi named Akiva who
was out in the village picking up supplies one day when he
absent-mindedly wandered the wrong way home. Suddenly
a voice cut through the fog, "Stop! Who are you and why are
you here?". Startled, he realized he'd wandered into the
Roman garrison, the voice coming from the young sentry
keeping guard.

Being a rabbi, he was good at answering questions by
asking them; "How much do they pay you to stand guard and
ask that question of all who approach?", he inquired.

Seeing that the intruder was a rabbi, the sentry softened and answered, "Five drachmas a week, sir". Fully aware of the value of those two questions, the rabbi offered to double his pay if he would accompany him home, stand in front of his cottage and ask him the same question each morning as he began his day: "Who are you, and why are you here?"

When was the last time you answered those questions? Who are you? And why are you here?

These questions are a little different from the ones we dug into in the last section (see Chapter 2: Ask Questions). While those tap into your passion, these start to uncover your purpose. Who you are and why you believe you're here will not only influence how you carry yourself and present yourself to the world, but the way in which you move through your days.

We're going to tackle this a little backwards, taking on the why here, and the who in the next chapter.

THERE MUST BE MORE

Think of the conversation between Alice and the Cheshire Cat in Lewis Carroll's 'Alice in Wonderland'. "Where are you going?", asks the cat. "Which way should I go?" responds the young Alice. "That depends on where you are going", he replies. "I don't know", the girl says. "Then it doesn't matter which way you go."

Much like Alice, many of us haven't a clue where we're going. We've become pretty adept at just going through the motions, doing what we've always done and getting what we've always gotten. But long before we even pause to search out the answer to 'why are you here', our hearts - with an unmistakable ache - betray our deeper need to know 'there must be more to life than this'.

We've all felt it. We've just not all taken the time to sit with it, to poke and prod it. And until we do, we'll have no inclination whatsoever to put any thought into which way we're going. We'll continue on autopilot until the next time the ache catches us off guard and we turn our ear toward the question.

When you know who you are, at your core, and have a pretty good idea of why you're here, your days will start to shift from blurry and haphazard, unfulfilled and monotonous, to focused, intentional and exciting. You'll begin seeing them for what they really are; brush-strokes on the larger canvas of your life.

As we search out and flesh out the answers to these questions, the picture starts to take shape. But you should know that the medium with which we're working is unlike any other. Rather than applying color to a blank canvas, it brings to life the picture that is already there. Each stroke removes more of the haze so that more of the masterpiece can shine through.

The canvas is really big and our brush is really small, and it will take thousands upon thousands of little strokes over the course of a lifetime to complete the picture, for this is the artwork of our lives. It is the answer to why we're here, and is just a small piece in the brilliant mosaic our Creator is shaping with humanity.

LIVING BACKWARDS

We are too close to this masterpiece of our lives to really get an idea of what it looks like. Our noses are pressed against the canvas. We see light and bright, and love those strokes. And we make out dark and harsh, and are not particularly fond of those ones.

While we see but a fragment of what lies ahead, we do have woven into the fabric of who we are, inklings of what the bigger picture might look like. Like a connect-the-dots project, each step and each stroke makes it clearer.

I believe a key to uncovering the artwork of our lives is found in looking ahead to the very end and spending a moment with our *legacy*. Our legacy is that which we pass on to others; so much more than a physical inheritance, it is the spiritual and emotional treasure we leave behind that others remember us by.

When we intentionally live with a legacy-centric mindset, it's as though we're taking ownership of our eulogy and declaring, "This is what I want to be remembered for. This shall be my battle cry and the anthem of my days so that when I'm gone there will be no question as to *why* I lived".

Think about your funeral for a moment; not with a bitter taste in your mouth, as if you died suddenly today - envision it rather through your 'ideal' lens. You've lived a long, full, influential life - the life you long to, and intend to, live. When it's all said and done, and the period has been placed on the story God wanted to write with the pen of your life, what would your funeral sound like?

...What would people say about you? About the way you lived? And loved? And spent yourself?

...What would you be remembered for?

...What would be the common thread shared throughout?

...Who were you, really? What were your core values, and how did you flesh those out?

...What did the way in which you lived your life say about what was most important to you?

...Why did you believe you were alive, and what did you do with that knowledge to make it evident to the lives around you?

Take a few minutes to really think about this. Don't rush this.

...What would the pastor say in opening the service?

...What few words would need to be said in order for everyone to think, "Aah yes, I'm at the right place! That was her alright!"?

...What would your spouse say?

...How about your children?

...What might your siblings say?

...What about your neighbors?

...And your colleagues?

...The homeless woman in your community?

...What about the people who show up at your funeral - whom you've never met - but whose lives were impacted by your work? Your words, your art, that project you started, that song you wrote. That life you lived.

This is your *legacy*. And it is a snippet of God's redemptive story, told through your life.

> *"I don't skate to where the puck is,*
> *I skate to where the puck is going to be"*
> *Wayne Gretzky*

LOOKING UP

Centuries ago in the early 1500s, a young sculptor was commissioned to paint the ceiling of a chapel. While it took 4 uncomfortable years, and inspired woeful poetry from the sculptor who was convinced his body was falling apart, and that he was officially in the wrong profession, Michelangelo left a masterpiece in Rome's Sistine Chapel.

Up until the 1980s, there were broad assumptions that the artist had intentionally chosen dark colors to depict the biblical scenes. But as experts started the painstaking process of restoring the ceiling to its original glory, which took longer to restore than to paint, they were surprised by the vibrancy of Michelangelo's work. He hadn't painted God and man in darker shades of melancholy, after all.

It was only after the careful removal of salt, grime and the smoke residue that had slowly taken up residence on the ceiling, that they discovered the dark haze was in fact an accumulation of soot that had built up over hundreds of years of candle-lit mass.

You see, God's purpose for your life is etched into the fabric of who you are, and it's utterly breath-taking. Our souls instinctively yearn to uncover it and flesh it out. Like the soot-caked masterpiece on the Sistine chapel's ceiling, or the black coated scratch art projects we did as kids, the image is all there - we just need to chip away at it to reveal the colorful design beneath.

Life is a journey of uncovering that design and only when we get to the end will we see and grasp the beauty of the full picture. We are typically too close to the canvas to take in the magnitude of it, but as we work to uncover it, asking ourselves often, 'who am I and why am I here?', we'll start to see a clearer and clearer image take shape.

EMBRACE THE PROCESS

When our kiddos were wee tykes, we would put their multivitamin gummies in front of them, just beyond their dinner plate, and remind them that those delicious little nuggets of rubberized nutrition were theirs as soon as they were finished. And let me tell you, they endured their broccoli and brussell sprouts for the joy of the gummies set before them.

If the completed picture is the prize of a purpose-driven life, daily life is the process. And the sooner we learn to embrace the process, the sooner we'll recognize the treasure hidden within the process itself.

Remember how the root word of 'passion' is suffering? When we have a vision for our lives that influences our every move, we will push through the momentary discomfort and suffering because the prize awaiting us is that valuable. The power of our 'why' woos us to the finish line.

Envisioning and journaling what you want your funeral to be like is like holding that magic scratch art piece up to the light. If you tilt it just slightly, you can see a faint image showing through. Taking this step applies an intentional, albeit faint, outline to the canvas of your life, and guides every stroke after it.

It pulls our focus out from within, to the people around us. It is a personal mission statement of sorts, reminding us that our lives aren't really about us in the first place. We're here for a much bigger purpose.

"Please think about your legacy,
Because you're writing it every day."
Gary Vaynerchuk

DIG DEEPER ON PAGE 31
OF THE STUDY GUIDE

CHAPTER 10

R | REDEFINE SUCCESS

" Success is the ability to go
from one failure to another
with no loss of enthusiasm"

WINSTON CHURCHILL

In an effort to plow straighter lines in his often chaotically harvested field, a farmer decided to fix his gaze on a large boulder in the distance and use it as a landmark. Off he went, back and forth, back and forth. After hours of plowing, his field was complete. But upon surveying his work, rather than straight lines, he found wavy ones. Baffled by the lack of consistency in his work he headed over to the boulder to assess the field from higher up.

While surprised by just how far south the boulder turned

out to be, he was more surprised to discover that the boulder was in fact a grazing ox in the neighboring field.

Success is a moving target. It waltzes around like a mirage, teasing us from the horizon, saying "just a little bit further, do just a little bit more, try a little harder". But it's always just beyond our reach.

REDEFINITION

We have defined success and failure in such black and white terms, deeming one good and desirable, and the other something of which we're quite terrified, so maybe it's time we redefined them. In seeing them as opposite ends of some cosmic measuring stick, we're missing out on the joy and growth of living life in the refreshing shades of grace between the two.

While we'll tackle the topic of failure in more depth in a few chapters, it's essential that we acknowledge the delicate dance it does with success throughout our lives. In seeing the two as no longer mutually exclusive, but rather beautifully interconnected, every issue we face becomes an opportunity for growth.

You've most likely heard the saying, "What would you do if you knew you couldn't fail?" Maybe we should be asking a better question; "What lines up with your personal mission so brilliantly that it would be worth doing even if it meant risking failure?"

Success is attractive, I get it. But we assume the more successful our lives become, the more satisfied and influential we become, and that's simply not true. That mentality is a fast track to burnout. It's easy to want to pour our effort into external accomplishment and the crushing of epic goals, because the results are more tangible. And we like tangible.

> The truth is, it doesn't matter how much you accumulate, accomplish or achieve on the outside, you will never feel like you're enough until you realize you're already enough on the inside.

There are not many things in life that scare me. I'm not a fan of snakes or scorpions, but they don't really scare me. I don't like big dogs, especially if they're running at me, and I loathe feeling foolish in public. And I mean lo-o-o-oathe. Occasionally reading the news strikes fear into me, but then I quickly remember why I don't read the news.

What does scare me, however, is the thought of wasting my life. The idea that I could throw all my energy and time and talent and resources into climbing that ladder...only to find it was leaning against the wrong wall. That at the end of my life God will show me snapshots of all the good things I accomplished with my life, but on another screen will flash all the things I could have done had I not been so preoccupied with some myopic definition of success. And that the second montage would be so much more substantial than the first. *That* scares me. And it drives me daily to examine my relationship with success.

"The pessimist complains about the wind; the optimist expects it to change; the realist adjusts the sails."
William Arthur Ward

I've always been a dreamer. And while I went through a dark season of the soul where hopelessness screamed louder than any dream could, I'm learning to dream again. Big audacious dreams. Getting older has not lessened my ability to dream, it has intensified it. It has enabled me to embrace the fact that while reality often doesn't pan out exactly the way I envision it will, it's even better in the end.

YOUR PURPOSE 2.0

One of my very favorite folktales is *The Tale of Three Trees*[17]. The story opens with 3 little trees sitting proudly on a mountaintop, dreaming of what they want to be when they grow up.

The first tree looks up at the twinkling stars and dreams of being turned into a beautiful treasure chest. The most beautiful in all the world.

The second tree looks out at the stream trickling nearby and declares its dream of one day becoming a mighty sailing ship, carrying Kings across wild waters. The strongest ship in all the world.

The third tree looks down at all the busy people going about their busy lives in the valley below and decides it wants to stay put. It dreams of being the tallest tree in all the world, catching people's attention and turning it heavenward.

Years pass and the trees grow big, all the while hoping and praying their dreams come true.

One day three woodcutters scale the mountain. Seeing the beauty of the first tree, a woodcutter swings his axe. "This is perfect to sell to a carpenter!", he declares. "Now I will be made into a treasure chest", thinks the tree, "holding glorious treasure!"

Seeing the strength of the second tree, the next woodcutter swings his axe. "This is perfect to sell to a shipyard", he declares. "Now I can carry Kings and sail those mighty waters", thinks the tree excitedly.

The third tree is heart-broken as the final woodcutter approaches her indifferently. "I'm sure I can use this at some point", he mutters. Mustering all her courage to stand up straight and tall one final time, the axe swings and her dreams of pointing people heavenward fall.

One by one the trees' dreams fade as they realize what they had hoped is not what's coming to pass.

The first tree is formed into a simple feed box and filled with hay for noisy farm animals. A far cry from a treasure chest filled with fortunes.

The second tree is fashioned into a simple fishing boat and taken to a small lake where she is used to haul smelly fish in to shore. A far cry from a mighty sailing ship carrying Kings.

The third tree is simply cut into sturdy beams and left in a heap of lumber. A far cry from her dream to simply stay erect, pointing to God.

Years pass and the three trees all but forget about the dreams they once had. I'll let the words of Angela Elwell Hunt carry you through the remainder of the story...

"But one night golden starlight poured over the first tree as a young woman placed her newborn baby in the feed box. "I wish I could make a cradle for him," her husband whispered. The mother squeezed his hand and smiled as the starlight shone on the smooth and sturdy wood. "This manger is beautiful", she said. And suddenly the first tree knew he was holding the greatest treasure in all the world.

One evening a tired traveler and his friends crowded into the old fishing boat. The traveler fell asleep as the second tree quietly sailed out into the lake. Soon a thundering and thrashing storm arose. The little tree shuddered. He knew he did not have the strength to carry so many passengers safely through the wind and rain. The tired man awakened. He stood up, stretched out his hand, and said, "Peace." The storm stopped as quickly as it had begun. And suddenly the second tree knew he was carrying the King of heaven and earth.

One Friday morning, the third tree was startled when her beams were yanked from the forgotten woodpile. She flinched as she was carried through an angry, jeering crowd. She shuddered when soldiers nailed a man's hand to her. She felt ugly and harsh and cruel. But on Sunday morning, when the sun rose and the earth trembled with joy beneath her, the third tree knew that God's love had changed everything. It had made the first tree beautiful. It had made the second tree strong. And every time people thought of the third tree, they would think of God. That was better than being the tallest tree in the world".

This sweet story so captured my heart the first time I heard it several years ago and has fast became a family favorite. I read it to my children at least once a year and, without fail, am undone during the final pages. I get full-body goosebumps. Not because of some crazy twist of tragedy woven into the end that I forgot about, but because the story of unexpectedly greater purpose moves me deeply each time.

It convicts, encourages and redefines "success" all at the same time. I am reminded that as much as I crave fruition for the things that bubble in my heart, that God has bigger dreams for those very things. That even when I'm wrestling with feelings of frustration, inadequacy or failure, God is weaving all things together, behind the scenes, for His purpose. And His plans trump mine every single time.

"I used to be afraid of failing at something that really mattered to me, but now I'm more afraid of succeeding at things that don't matter"
Bob Goff

HEART OVER HUSTLE

While some are content to haphazardly meander their way through life, others hustle hard and go after the gold. They set their sights on their desired outcome, drop their heads and push, only to find - when they "arrive" - that it wasn't all it cracked up to be. Or that in their ruthless determination to get there, it cost them more than they realized.

If you're a particularly driven, goal-oriented person, the lure of success speaks your language and the draw is powerful. But it is crucial that we pause often to lift our heads and re-evaluate our position and course. The thought of throwing myself fully into something, sacrificing mightily along the way, only to find I've reached the top of the wrong thing utterly terrifies me. Without thoughtful pauses along the way, to reevaluate and seek outside wisdom, we run the risk of succeeding at the wrong things and missing out on what really matters.

There is a big difference between 'being a success' and 'making an impact'.

As John Maxwell so stunningly describes in his new book, *Intentional Living: Choosing a Life That Matters*, once you've learned to live intentionally, seeking significance over success, experiencing success alone will not be enough. He describes success as typically being self-centric, where we work to add value to ourselves, while significance is all about adding value to others. I love this distinction, and strive to live out the latter. Being 'otherly', after all, is at the heart of our personal mission statement.

"The purpose of life is to live it, to taste experience to the utmost, to reach out eagerly and without fear for newer and richer experience."
Eleanor Roosevelt

THE POWER OF PERSPECTIVE

I have spent much of my adult life fluctuating between working toward big, audacious dreams, with hope bubbling and wheels turning, and wanting to throw in the towel and assume the fetal position. I didn't have many big, audacious dreams or aspirations as a teenager. I just wanted to be liked and not feel like an idiot in public. Of course I wanted to succeed at something, but I couldn't have told you for the life of me what that was.

My inability to vision-cast was crippled somewhat by a very warped sense of self. But I think the thing that hindered me most was the zoomed-in perspective I had of my life. I couldn't see the forest for the trees, or rather, I couldn't see the big picture for the crooked paintbrush in my hand.

I cannot tell you how much our perspective matters. As we've discovered in previous chapters, stepping back from the canvas to examine the whole allows us to see things we miss when our heads are down, pedal to the metal.

We all long to live lives that matter. That count for something. We crave significance because we were hard-wired both to need it and to cultivate it. To make a positive impact on the world around us.

That deep longing you have to matter isn't silly, it isn't narcissistic, and it isn't unrealistic. It's a homing device divinely embedded in your DNA to woo you toward the life you were created for.

When we're open to the potential wrapped up in the many twists and turns and detours along the way, not to mention the occasional recalibration of the course altogether, we can move through life with a far greater sense of purpose even when things play out differently than we'd envisioned.

It is essential that we listen to and honor our longing to make a difference with this one precious life we have. Critical to the fleshing out of that longing is the determination to not package it neatly into a little box and wrap it up with the bow of superficial success.

"What counts in life is not the mere fact that we have lived. It is what difference we have made to the lives of others that will determine the significance of the life we lead"
Nelson Mandela

DIG DEEPER ON PAGE 33
OF THE STUDY GUIDE

CHAPTER 11

P | PULL THOSE WEEDS

"A bird sitting on a tree is never afraid of the branch breaking, because her trust is not in the branch but in her own wings."

UNKNOWN

The circus had come to town and the elephants were Sadie's favorite. They always were. Whether it was their long trunks, big ears or their snuffaluffagus eyelashes, she wasn't certain, but something about these docile giants mesmerized her.

When they visited the elephant tent after the performance, it didn't take her long to notice the chains. All three of the famous performing elephants were now standing still, shackled by their rear left leg. Seemingly unperturbed by their restraint, she inquired as to its purpose.

"That's how we keep them from running away, young lady", the man explained.

That answer did not suffice. Averaging 10 feet tall and 12,000 pounds, and capable of snapping a tree in two like we would snap a toothpick, it seemed absurd that these beasts would be held by such a flimsy chain. "But how does that little chain hold such a big elephant?", she pried.

"Well, when they were just little babies, this is how we trained them. They couldn't break the chains then, and if they tried really hard, the metal would dig into their leg and wouldn't feel very good, so they would just stop trying. Now they're big and tall and so very strong, but they've grown to believe that they can't break the chain. They learned quickly that it hurts when they try, so they just don't try any more".

"The only thing that stands in between you and your dreams is the will to try and the belief that it is actually possible."
Joel Brown

We encounter chains of our own throughout our lives. Some are vocal and blatant, while others are so small and far off in the distance that it's hard to identify them. They're just visible enough to remind us of our incapability. These restraints hold us captive, threatening pain and discomfort if we push the boundary line.

THE BARK AND THE BITE

These chains we've grown accustomed to dragging around with us seem awfully fierce at first glance, and yet when examined up close, are flimsy and fragile. They are faulty belief systems that keep us tethered to an old way of thinking. Built on an unspoken belief that if something was true for us in that moment, be it in our formative years or in an emotionally vulnerable season, it must be true now. While we don't actively choose to think this way, and may not even be able to identify limiting beliefs at first, we all have them.

They sprout the fruit of their twisted roots everywhere, from the bedroom to the boardroom...

"My value and worth depend on others' ability to recognize it. If I'm not in a serious relationship, I am all alone. If I'm not being pursued, I am unwanted."

"Perfection is necessary, mistakes are unacceptable. I cannot make a mistake because it will mean that I am unacceptable."

"I will lose the respect of others if I fail. So I will stay safe, even if it means I remain miserable. I will remain comfortable, even if it means not doing what I long to do. Risking failure is not an option."

"If someone disagrees with me, they are personally attacking me. Conflict is bad. They are highlighting my incompetence. I've been found out as the fraud that I believe I am."

"I've tried and I've failed. I always fail. I will never kick this bad habit. I'll never succeed in developing that new habit. What's the point in trying?"

"I can't celebrate her and champion her dreams. If she succeeds, it means I won't be able to. If she really shines, I'll look dull in comparison. There's not enough to go around, we can't all win."

These belief systems have their tendrils anchored in previous experiences where lies took root in our vulnerable state, and they have grown into fully-blown tethers fashioned from fear and shame. While their bark is distinctly more threatening than their bite, all we know is that they were strong enough to hold us hostage then, and they still hold us now. So we hack away at the weeds that keep popping up and wrapping themselves around our ankles, but until we dig down deep and deal with the roots, we're just managing the symptoms.

GETTING OUR HANDS DIRTY

My greatest limitations were based around fear of looking foolish, of failing, and of being rejected. While I had worked through a great deal of personal baggage, I found myself tugging at some pretty hefty vocation-related chains last year. These ones were all tied to my work performance and creative identity, and exposed a deep root of inadequacy.

Because of having experienced life under the crippling weight of shame, only to discover a freedom that had been mine for the taking throughout those 7 excruciating years, I have become obsessed with freedom. Quite literally obsessed. If I identify an area of my life where lies are taking root or faulty belief systems are at work, I sniff them out like a bloodhound. I weed the soil of my heart frequently, searching for things that need to go. I'm just not interested in spending another day of my life carrying unnecessary baggage or being held back from the life I'm called to. No ma'am. Not interested.

Please don't confuse my self-awareness with being a fear-monger or a witch-hunter. They are worlds apart. I'm not interested in finding things that aren't there in an effort to blame them for bad behavior, nor am I interested in wasting time digging in dirt that's not mine to dig in. I'm not a negative person, in fact I find negativity suffocates my soul. I don't go looking for it nor am I interested in manufacturing it. But if something ugly rears its head in my heart or mind, no matter how messy my hands have to get to uproot it, you better believe it's being evicted.

Having close friends and mentors who are both authentic and bold has helped to create an environment where pulling these weeds is celebrated. Rather than hide them when they sprout, we help identify them in each other and celebrate their uprooting.

I have stumbled upon several of these limiting beliefs over the past few years and have been working intentionally to dismantle them.

Last year, while sitting on the beach with my dear friend and mentor, Cindra, we unearthed a big one. I had poured out my heart to her about how stuck I felt, when she turned to me and declared, "That's a big one, girlfriend! I think you might want to talk to Carol about that". Ah yes, *Carol*. This was the equivalent of someone saying, "This is above my pay-grade...it's time to bring in the big guns."

While this mutual friend of ours is an incredibly kind, wise woman, the reason she was mentioned was not for additional friendship support. No, it was a "professional help" suggestion. Carol, alongside her hubby, are counselors whose life's passion is helping people find freedom from the lies and limiting beliefs that hold them captive. It takes a good friend to acknowledge when reinforcements are necessary.

I started meeting with Carol, oddly excited to confront this monstrous beast of inadequacy that had taken up residence in the shadows of my heart. I'd been tripping over this thing for longer than I could recall and its roots had become so deeply interwoven with different areas of my life that I didn't know where to start digging. Over a period of a few months, we talked and prayed and worked through the dirt, unearthing the taproot beneath some of my biggest struggles.

"Aerodynamically the bumblebee shouldn't be able to fly, but the bumblebee doesn't know that so it goes on flying anyway."
Mary Kay Ash

Understand that I didn't have a single 'business bone' in my body when I started out 9 years ago. As I often joke (and don't be fooled, it's 100% true), I have Googled my way through everything from how to use design software, how to code a website, and how to deliver an extraordinary presentation, to how to publish a book and how to not suck while doing it all.

If there was any area of my life that inadequacy could sneak in and take over, it was this one. I felt fiercely out of my league and was beginning to feel the ache in my neck from having my cheek pressed up against the glass ceiling for so long. I could see what I wanted but I didn't know how to get there. Unfortunately, you can't Google your way through ceiling smashing and limiting belief shattering.

Add a severe case of 'impostor syndrome', with its signature fear of being found out as a fraud, and I was stuck fast.

But Carol and Cindra, along with the amazing business women I've met with weekly over the past year, have helped me fashion a truth-tipped jackhammer and together we have shattered that ceiling. As I continue to guard my mind and plant truth where lies once grew, I am tasting the sweet freedom that comes from breaking the chain.

WHAT HOLDS US

I have processed through several limiting beliefs, and the downhill spiral of thoughts that accompany them, over the past year. I want to share a few of them with you in the hopes that they might help you identify your own. And yes, you'll fully understand why I needed counseling after reading these.

"If that important person doesn't respond to my email,

they're rejecting me. If I don't get picked for that opportunity, they're rejecting me. If no one reads and responds to what I wrote, or celebrates what I created, they're rejecting my work, so they're rejecting an expression of me. If I put myself out there - and nothing happens - not only will I look like a fool, but it will be another rejection. Because I am rejected so often, there must be something inherently wrong with me. I am broken, unworthy and incapable of succeeding."

"Handling money is so uncomfortable for me. It was so easy for me to create that, and I love what I do, so I feel bad charging them for it. What if I charge them and they don't think what I delivered was worth it? I'm greedy if I want to make money for something that feels so easy and fun. Besides, I wouldn't pay someone to do that - I could just do it myself - so I can't charge them full price. And people really like me if I keep giving myself away for free. I just have to keep my weariness and resentment in check, it's good to be generous. Gosh, I'm so unprofessional. I'll never earn a living doing this".

"Oh my gosh, she's so amazing. Between her talent and her massive following and her crazy perfect hair, I'll never be able to compete with that. There's no room for me at the table. Every seat has already been taken by some ridiculously gifted woman, and here I stand, awkward wallflower in the corner. I should probably bow out gracefully while I still can."

It seems silly to sit back and read these now. In fact, it's tempting to linger on the back space button and remove all evidence of their presence in my thinking. But here's why I won't: because it's of utmost importance that we understand the power of these little commentaries that play over and over again in our minds, forming link after link in the chain.

Each time I sat in that chair, I was faced with the opportunity to contrast what I knew was true, intellectually and theologically, with what I felt was true, cognitively and experientially.

I slowly began to see that while those closest to me wholeheartedly believed I was capable of accomplishing something extraordinary, I was quite certain I was not. I was, in fact, convinced I was doomed to flounder. Intrinsically defective. I had a long list of reasons why I was the least likely candidate in the world to succeed, and 3 rehearsed lines about why, just maybe, God could use even a wreck like me. Maybe, some day.

It's baffling when you look back at things you've believed for so long, with a little bit of distance between you and them (in this case, only a few months), and are utterly gob smacked that you fell for them for so long. Utter growth-hindering, wing-clipping hogwash was what it was. To think of all the things I could have accomplished had I not been so afraid. Of failure, of rejection, or of looking foolish.

But I am convinced that even this will eventually be redeemed.

"We will all struggle and fall, we will know what it means to be both brave and brokenhearted"
Brené Brown

When we live for so long, paralyzed by fear, we can forget that we were created to move freely, bravely, and confidently through life. Our self-established limitations become boundary-lines we do not cross. It hurts too much to resist the chain. We become fiercely risk-averse and comfort-zone protective.

Over time we stop fighting for full range of motion - in our marriages, in our businesses, in our circles of influence - because we start believing that not only is it impossible, but that it's actually how we were designed to operate.

Eventually we silence the ache for more and go about our lives on auto-pilot, in quiet desperation.

But freedom is a God ordained birth-right, sweet friend, and it came at an incredibly high price.

You know that saying, "not my circus, not my monkeys"? Well, they may not be your monkeys - or elephants in this case - but this is your circus. Until, that is, you walk free. Living fully depends on you breaking those chains; that stinkin'-thinkin' that holds you hostage.

The good news is this: if you're brave enough to examine them and confront them, you'll discover their ability to hold you boils down to your willingness to believe that they can. They are only as strong as you choose to believe they are.

Here's the thing we need to understand: we can have the whole world rooting for us, and have acquired every necessary skill in the book, but at the end of the day our ability to stick it out through the turbulence of life and truly fulfill what we were created to do has little do to with what others think of us and everything to do with what we believe about ourselves.

"I can do all this through him who gives me strength."
Philippians 4:13

DIG DEEPER ON PAGE 35
OF THE STUDY GUIDE

CHAPTER 12

O | OVERFLOW THE INPUT

"The purpose of life is not to be
happy. It is to be useful, to be
honorable, to be compassionate,
to have it make some difference
that you have lived and lived well"

RALPH WALDO EMERSON

Between the neighboring countries of Israel and Jordan, you'll find the Jordan River which flows south from Lake Huleh into the Sea of Galilee. This sea, which is really more like a lake, is beautiful and vibrant, teeming with marine life. It is a hub of activity, both in the water and around its shores.

About 65 miles due south, in a deep valley, we find the Dead Sea. Fed by the exact same source as the Sea of

Galilee, it could not be more opposite. With a salt content of 33%, 8 times higher than other seas, life simply does not exist here. It cannot.

One is lush and green, the other stark and sterile. If these two bodies of water are fed by the same source, what makes them so incredibly different? Well, the Sea of Galilee receives water from the Jordan River, and then passes it along. The other only receives.

With no outlet, the Dead Sea loses water only through evaporation, leaving it with its high levels of salinity and no life.

In this chapter we're tackling the topic of mentoring, or more broadly, the need to have both wise, life-giving input flowing in and wise, life-giving output flowing out of our lives. We need to be mentored, and we need to mentor. And yes, you do have what it takes.

Your willingness to pour into others is what makes you the perfect candidate, it's not about being an expert or having the ability to appear like you have it all together that qualifies you to mentor someone.

And if you're not yet willing, I trust that by the end of this chapter, you will be.

"Listen to advice and accept discipline, and
at the end you will be counted among the wise."
Proverbs 19:20

WALKING TOGETHER

I have been fortunate enough to walk alongside some phenomenally wise women over the past two decades. They have sown into my marriage, my spiritual life, my motherhood journey, my mental and emotional health, and my business ventures through their wise counsel and faithful encouragement. They have lifted my chin, called me out and mined gold I didn't know was there.

While scattered over twenty years and rarely having any connection to each other, God has used their input in my life to bring about an astounding level of growth and maturity in just the right way at just the right time. The way he orchestrated their input astounds me. And while their presence in my life has been a blessing I can credit God alone for, my willingness to walk honestly and vulnerably with them has been essential to that growth. As Amos 3:3 asks, "do two walk together unless they have agreed to do so?".

While there have been seasons that I have not actively had a "mentor", because of the different circles we intentionally and actively move in, I know exactly where to find one when I need one. Refer back to the 'Surround Yourself' chapter if you need a refresher on the importance of cultivating authentic friendship with quality people and the joy of finding your tribe.

ARE YOU MY MENTOR?

I cannot think of a time in my adult life when the woman, or women, that mentored me weren't already rubbing shoulders with me in some capacity. In other words, I did not seek out a mentor I didn't already know or have some type of connection with, and most often our mentoring relationship developed naturally out of our already existing friendship, fledgling as it may have been at the time. Some of them were more official mentoring relationships, initiated with the sometimes awkward question, "Would you be willing to mentor me for a season?", while others grew organically into that type of relationship which we together then simply nurtured. It is often in hindsight that I recognize the extent to which those friends fulfilled their mentoring role in my life.

The word mentor means different things to different people, but here's how I'm loosely defining the mentoring relationship; a trusting relationship in which a more experienced person comes alongside a less experienced one to cultivate growth through encouragement, insight, counsel and honest feedback.

Someone once described a mentor as a person whose hindsight can become your foresight. I love that definition. It speaks to the willingness to simply share life and the lessons learned along the way, with another.

If we want to grow and develop as women and as leaders, we have got to seek out those who are wiser, more mature and further along than we are on the journey.

> The key here is to find wise, savvy women who are both brutally honest and extraordinarily gracious, and then walk alongside them.

Mentoring relationships create a safe place to get honest feedback and sometimes hard-to-swallow insight. It really is far more simple than we tend to make it. Spend time with them, learn from them, and be willing to get out of your comfort zone with them. Give them full permission to ask you hard questions, and then ask them tough questions in return.

Ask them to hold you accountable. Despite the unpleasant connotation this word carries, especially in the church, it is so important that we understand that accountability is a gift. It is, after all, simply giving an account of one's ability. When we hold someone accountable we're essentially calling that person up to the level of greatness of which they are capable. We're saying, "You *are able* and I'm going to hold you to it!". Accountability was never intended to be a knuckle-thumping session; it was designed to remind us that we were made for more.

There have been seasons in my life that all I've needed was for someone to come alongside me and remind me that while it wasn't going to be easy, it sure was going to be worthwhile. As a mom, as a wife, as a child of God, and as a business owner. This is one of the greatest gifts our mentors give us; brutal honesty wrapped in hope. Truth sandwiches laced with grace.

Know that while great friends and great mentors may overlap, they are *not* the same thing. Your best friend is most likely not your mentor, nor should she ever be. Not all friendships can handle the type of gut-level honesty and parental-style accountability that mentorship requires. Because it can put a strain on the relationship, it's often avoided.

In the mentoring relationship, this level of input is not only expected, but treasured and appreciated. This is not to say your mentor might not become a great friend (they almost always do), or as in my case, that my mom - who is one of my dearest friends – doesn't often play the role of mentor in my life. With this in mind, it's important to not dismiss the need for a mentor in the name of already having girlfriends. We need both friends and mentors.

"Getting the most out of life isn't about how much you keep for yourself but how much you pour into others"
David Stoddard

AND THEN IT FLOWS OUT

Much like the Sea of Galilee, in order to stay healthy and vibrant we need to make sure we have output along with the input. Along with the wisdom and guidance we receive, we need to be intentionally pouring out into others.

> This is usually the part where I get to deal with big buts.
> But I am not old enough...wise enough...smart enough.
> But I'm not experienced enough... perfect enough...
>   confident enough.
> But I'm not...(insert your inadequacy here).

Allow me to clear up a couple of things:

To be a mentor you do not have to be...a bona-fide old woman, a degree holding company president or a self-proclaimed expert. And you don't have to pretend as though you have it all together.

You have only to be willing, committed, and one step ahead. Willing to share what you *do* know with someone who doesn't yet know what you know, and be committed to seeing them grow. Not necessarily succeed - as that is up to *them* - but grow.

Being generous with our time, knowledge and resources is as critical to our own health and growth as surrounding ourselves with women who extend those same things to us.

When I got my first DSLR camera a few years ago, several women commented on the photographs I was posting on my blog and asked me to teach them how to use their cameras. I laughed every time I heard it because it seemed ludicrous to "instruct" others when I was still trying to figure it out myself. But they persisted. So I gathered the information I had found, compiled all the resources I had found helpful, and hosted a little get together at my house. We drank coffee, ate munchies, and worked our way through the little 'Photography 101' handout I'd created, then played with our cameras together. We had so much fun and they all found it helpful and inspiring.

This teach-while-I-learn thing has become somewhat of a trend. Shortly after I opened my online store, women asked to meet for coffee and glean some insight on how to start a business and sell their products. A few weeks after I started playing with watercolor paint, I was asked to teach a community painting class. Earlier this year I taught an online class through the Influence Network[18] on the art of writing and self-publishing.

I tell you this not to say, "tra-la-la, look at me!", but so you'll understand: I had no clue what I was doing. Or rather, I felt as though I had no clue what I was doing. I knew just a few basics and a couple of tips and tricks and, as it turns out, there were some gals a few steps behind me who knew even less than I did.

If I wait until I know it all and feel completely confident...I'm confident I'll never do it. We've got to tap into the Nike spirit here and "just do it".

TEACH WHILE YOU LEARN

I tend to get hung up on all the people way far ahead of me. They know what they're doing. They're über successful. They're the experts. Who am I to teach people?

While I'm fully aware of the fact that there is still so much to learn on any subject, I'm learning to shift my gaze off the horizon where all the brilliant folk hang out, and look back over my shoulder to the people a few steps behind me. Instead of wallowing in "What do I know?", I'm asking myself, "Who would benefit from what I do know?".

Each and every time I'm asked to share what I'm learning while I'm still learning it my instinct is to laugh it off and say, "What! Me? I haven't a clue what I'm doing...trust me, there are WAY smarter people out there that can help you". Sometimes that's busyness talking, because I haven't a clue where I'll squeeze them into an already overflowing schedule, but most of the time I just feel inadequate and fearful of being exposed as not actually knowing as much as they think I do.

But here's the truth. We all know a thing or two about a thing or two, and there will always be someone further behind us on the path. In the same way you value what you glean from those ahead of you on the path, you have something to share with those a few steps behind you.

When we refuse to take our eyes off all the stuff we don't yet know, we're unable to use what we do know to help those even newer to the practice than we are.

This is after all how the Sea of Galilee stays healthy...in, through and then out.

If we're willing to get over ourselves and our need to feel accomplished and confident before we share the nuggets we know, we'll find there are women eager to come alongside us and grow. I think our human hunger for fellowship is also a factor here. Grow and connect? Yes please!

I've found this to be true in every single area of my life. And I'm learning to be brave and extend my offering, even if it's not the best version available. This is all a part of doing life together. You teach me what you know, and I'll teach you.

Someone will share her resources with you, while you offer your wisdom on the subjects you're passionate about with me. And around it flows.

The beautiful thing about being willing to teach what you know is that you learn more in the process.

My husband and I have mentored married couples and pre-marriage couples for almost ten years. And you should know...we've only been married for just over twelve years. We don't do it because we think we have it all together or because we're experts on the topic (we're not, just to clarify), nor do we have some fancy degree in marriage counseling. We're simply passionate about the subject, have incredible tools that were given to us when we were preparing for marriage, and because we have a story to tell.

When you look at it this way, we almost have an obligation to share what we know. If we have simple tools in our marriage tool belt, that others helped put there, that have helped us forge a strong healthy marriage - it would be wrong to keep them to ourselves and not share them with others who might desperately need them.

We also mentor couples because they keep seeking us out and asking us to. It amazes me really. We've walked with couples through marriage preparation, affairs, addictions, and profound loss. Not because we have it all together and our marriage is perfect, but because we're willing to walk through the mess of real life with couples because of the hope we've found in the midst of our own mess. And because, as all God-centric things do, it gives our own marriage a surge of life to invest in others.

Each and every time we're actively mentoring or teaching a class together, there's an added sweetness in our own relationship because loving on others - together - deepens our own bond and awakens something new in us.

CHANGING THE NARRATIVE

Apart from the role mentors have played in my life, I have a deep respect and gratitude for the men who have mentored my husband throughout his life. There is one in particular that I squeeze a little longer every time I get to see him. In a way I feel the sweetness of my marriage, and the solid foot it started out on, is in part thanks to him and his wise counsel. My life - and our marriage - could have looked very different.

If you know anything about my personal journey[19], you'll know that I've walked a colorful road, and that my heart took up residence in the dark because of one particular season. Shame drove me into hiding, and fear of being found out kept me there. I became an expert mask-wearer. I met my husband a few years after God really started to get a hold of my heart, but rather than work through all that brokenness, I stuffed it into invisible suitcases that I then dragged quietly around with me. I mastered the art of charm, creating the perfect illusion of being happy and healthy. No one knew I was imploding on the inside and for seven years I hid my past.

Long story short, two months before our wedding it all came spilling out. In a tearful, snotty mess. He sat there, dumbfounded by what he had just heard. So much pain. So much brokenness. So many lies.

But here's why I'm sharing a snapshot of this story with you; what this 22-year-old boy did next changed the course of our lives.

How easily he could have just walked away. Surely there was a purer finger for that ring?

Who would have blamed him for seeking comfort and consolation from his work buddies, who would have insisted he not take that from a girl and to drop me like a hot rock. Real men don't take that type of nonsense. No ma'am.

He could have gone to his parents who, rightfully so, would have felt incredible anger for what I had done to their son and might have advised him to end the relationship. It's only natural to pick up the offense of our loved ones, right?

But he didn't. He immediately sought counsel from his mentor. This spiritual father figure listened, comforted, and then urged him to check himself first. "Joe, are you perfect? Have you ever messed up in this area? It took incredible bravery for her to come to you. Promise me this, son...you two will work through this now and then you will never bring it up again".

Oh, friend. *This*. This counsel changed the course of my life. It was grace drenched in wisdom, wisdom soaked in grace. And had my husband not sought it, how different our marriage would look - if it would have even existed - today.

Not once in twelve years has he used my past as a weapon to shame or wound me. In fact, the very thing I feared would destroy us has become a primary platform for us to minister and mentor other couples.

Needless to say, the art of mentoring is dear to my heart, both in the personal and the professional realm.

> "Mentoring is a brain to pick, an ear to listen,
> and a push in the right direction"
> *John C. Crosby*

WE ALL COME ALIVE

Can you imagine how vibrant and healthy our communities would be if we were all willing to reach out and courageously give of ourselves to each other, imperfect and ill-equipped as we may feel? Generously sharing our time, our talent, our knowledge and our stories with each other, in a pulsating network of give-and-take. Seriously. The thought makes me giddy!

Whether it's wisdom for raising responsible teenagers, easy ways to freshen up your Wordpress site, or the best cleaning methods you've learned in your 15 years as a high school janitor, we need you. If you're especially good at managing money, or have a knack for planning and preparing freezer meals, we need you. If you know what it's like to navigate the harrowing waters of parenting a Type 1 diabetic child with grace and resilience, we need you. If you've climbed the corporate ladder and have tips for leading teams with integrity and authenticity, we need you.

Whoever you are, whatever you do and wherever you do it, we need you to show up and share yourself with us. To bring your little fish and loaves, if you will, and feed the people with what you have.

The combination of your unique experience and knowledge mixed with your distinct delivery method and style sets you up to touch a group of women in a way that only you can. It's a package deal, girlfriend, and there are young women aching to get their hands on that package. Don't keep it to yourself for fear of it not being good enough. It is good enough. *You* are good enough.

I understand that it can be terrifying. 'Insecure' has been my middle name for most of my life. But as I've stepped out and given what I do have to offer, that offering has grown, along with my courage.

There's nothing quite like using your influence - small as it may be - to encourage, equip and inspire others. We get to mine the gold out of them; what could possibly be more rewarding?

Mentoring relationships, accompanied by vibrant soul-sister connections, are the richest soil we could grow in.

Surround yourself with people who believe in the power of your dreams, and then find those whose dreams you can breathe life into. It's all about input and output, and we need to intentionally cultivate both in our relationships. It's like walking through life with our hands linked; one hand reaches forward, firmly planted in the hand of an older, wiser woman, and one hand reaches back, to guide and encourage someone who's a few steps behind.

> *"We make a living by what we get,*
> *but we make a life by what we give"*
> *Winston Churchill*

DIG DEEPER ON PAGE 37
OF THE STUDY GUIDE

CHAPTER 13

S | STUDENT STATUS

> "Anyone who stops learning is
> old, whether at twenty or
> eighty. Anyone who keeps
> learning stays young."
>
> HENRY FORD

One thousand four hundred and forty.

It's not the amount of money in my savings account. It's not the number of marbles my son owns, although considering the amount I step on throughout the day, sometimes I wonder. And it's not the number of friends I have on Facebook.

It's the number of minutes that make up a day. Every single day, for each and every one of us.

Our relationship with time is an interesting one. We've all experienced days that flew by at break-neck speed, and we've all endured that day that never.seemed.to.end. While there are many factors that influence how fast or slow our days seem to move - we all have exactly the same amount of time to spend every day.

It's true. Mother Teresa never managed to milk an extra minute out of her daily bank account, nor did that slacker kid in high school find a way to abbreviate theirs.

MAXIMIZING YOUR DASH

Not one of us knows how many days we are afforded here on earth. This time, tucked between our date of birth and date of death, is often referred to as the 'dash' (think of a tombstone). While our entrances and exits are entirely out of our control, what we choose to do with our lives in the in-between is completely up to us. We may have no say as to where we're born, and who our parents are, and little influence when it comes to how our family unit functions in the earlier years of life, however we do get to make choices as to what we will do with those experiences.

And when it comes to fleshing out our purpose, where even the worst of experiences have the potential to become stories of hope for someone else, this is good news!

Your time is precious. Along with your energy it is your most valuable and limited resource, and can accomplish extraordinary things when invested wisely.

Some of my favorite stories are dramatic accounts of determination and resilience in the face of fierce opposition, when failure seemed inevitable. While I'm often put off by 'rags to riches' hype, I'm wildly inspired by people who, against all odds, accomplished great things that then influence the lives of others and impact the world for good. They always remind me of the astounding value of our time. That every single minute counts.

I tend to treat my minutes like I do pennies. Or stray bobby pins. They're insignificant and worthless...until I desperately need one.

We don't realize how long a minute really is until we're stuck at a traffic light and our child's recital starts in 2 minutes. Or when we're holding a squat for 60 excruciating seconds.

I started doing daily handstands at the beginning of the year, first against random walls around the house, and finally on the threshold between the dining room and the living room. My toes just catch the lip of the partial wall that dips down from the ceiling, so it's the perfect place to stay erect and not have to lean against something to stay up, which makes for good form. I started on January 1st, staying up for twelve seconds, and just recently have been able to stay inverted for an entire minute. Emphasis on *entire* because it makes it sound much longer than it is. If there's such a thing as a 'hot second', then this is a 'painfully long minute'.

If we all have the same amount of time in a day, how is it that some accomplish astonishing feats, while others simply convert oxygen to carbon dioxide? Is it really just because some people are driven personalities with laser focus? You know, the ones harnessing their energy and funneling it into mad goal-crushing and name-taking? And that others are, well...just not?

Are some luckier than others? More fortunate and "privileged"? Are they smarter or more naturally energetic than those who don't seem to accomplish much in their lifetimes?

> Could it be that some people simply have a firmer grasp on the value of their time and the direct connection between their use of it and the impact their lives will have?

What I love most about this thinking being the dividing line - which I personally believe it is - is that it means everyone has the potential to change their lives.

...It's not about having no motivation, it's about getting into action first and building the momentum it takes to feel motivated.

...It's not about being the most talented, it's all about how you use what talent you already have.

...It's not about being too tired, it's about believing in the power of your dreams enough to take care of yourself in order to make it happen that becomes the only option.

...It's not about lack of knowledge, it's about figuring out where you need to go, and who you need to come alongside, so as to learn what you must do to make what matters happen.

At the end of the day, it's not about luck. It never has been. It's all about how you choose to use your time.

THE POWER OF CHOICE

When we forget how powerful we are, we don't bring that power into our everyday choices. Our time becomes something to be endured, rather than a bank account full of fresh opportunities. We tend to stop playing the game of chess and become a pawn in someone else's game. I don't want life to happen to me, I want to happen to my life.

I'm sure you've heard the tale of the old Cherokee who described his internal struggle to his young grandson as two wolves caught in a bag. One wolf represented fear, anger, jealousy and pride, the other representing love, goodness, compassion and faith.

After thinking about it for a moment, the young boy asks his grandfather, "Which wolf wins?".

"The one you feed" is his simple response.

And the answer remains that simple today. We have got to be so very careful about what we're feeding in our lives, because every single choice we make - or don't make - feeds something. And if we don't intentionally feed the right ones, we'll inadvertently feed the wrong ones.

I cannot tell you how many times I've heard, "Where do you find the time to do that?", followed by something to the effect of, "Oh, I don't have the time for that!". The thing is, we all have the same amount of time in a day. And last time I checked, nobody had 'found' any additional minutes stashed in a treasure chest in the wall. One thousand four hundred and forty minutes. We just choose to spend it differently.

And every reason I hear to the contrary, apart from the exhaustingly busy seasons of early parenting, mental or chronic illness, caring for children with special needs, or tending to aging parents, boil down to this: choice.

We choose our job. We choose our house, and house payment. We choose our spouse. We choose our hobbies. We choose our children's extracurricular activities. We choose our friends. We choose how much time to spend with our families. We choose our boundaries. We choose our television shows. We choose what to fuel our bodies with. And we choose what our schedule will look like.

Problems arise when people don't realize that they're choosing what their lives will look and feel like by how they choose all of these things...and so they don't intentionally choose the best things.

When we've taken the time to consider what type of legacy we want to leave, and choose to live from our eulogy backwards, our choices - both big and small - will line up with that ultimate goal. Because, as we'll discover in the next section, it's the small things we do consistently that become our habits, which then make up our lives, which weave together the threads of our legacy.

If we could see the impact our seemingly insignificant daily decisions have on the big picture, we would steward our time more wisely.

*"She turned her can'ts into cans
and her dreams into plans."*
Kobi Yamada

THE SCHOOL OF LIFE

I've heard it said that poor people have big televisions and rich people have big libraries. While I have nothing against big televisions, I am concerned by the lack of reading done by my generation and consequently by the next. Black words on white pages no longer cut it in this flashy, technology-driven world. We seem to have lost our appetite for nutritionally-dense education in favor of cheap, easily accessible entertainment. And I'm not referring to formal education.

Our information diet often resembles our nutritional diet: junk. And the adage holds true here: junk in, junk out.

Now don't get me wrong. All work and no play does indeed make Jane a dull girl, but even our play can have a purpose, and a richer one at that. Although I'm still trying to figure out how Netflix marathons of Blue Bloods can enrich my life. Maybe it counts for memorable hubby time and police culture education? [knuckle bumps]

My husband and I are intentional about carving out time for friendship, rest and fun because we're aware of the effect it has on our marriage, our family, our community, and even our work when those essential elements are missing.

We love movies. And I say love, I mean *lurve*. There's nothing quite like relaxing on our heinies with a cup of tea and some good convo. We love to sleep in on occasion, allowing Netflix to parent our children on Saturday mornings. Don't judge.

We're most certainly not Type A personalities. In fact I've often lamented my predisposition to laziness. I am totally down with being sedentary. It makes drinking multiple cups of tea in one sitting more possible. But, with that being said, we have a clear picture of what we want to accomplish with our lives, and that is what tears us from the sofa. We have big picture goals and small picture habits in place.

We also have seasons of laziness and lethargy where we completely lack motivation, focus and in some ways, even a sense of hope. Sometimes it's just one of us, and occasionally we've been down at the same time. That's no joke [#thestruggleisreal]. But we come out of them eventually, reevaluate and get moving. It's natural to fluctuate and ride the rollercoaster of motivation, we just have to keep showing up and doing what we know we have to until we're able to push through the barriers and forge onward.

"A teachable spirit is being willing to be a student in any areas you lack, to seek out knowledge and truth, in order to grow in humility, wisdom and excellence."
Holly Noel

IT'S UP TO YOU

You see, it really isn't about having time. It's all about whether we want something badly enough. Our lives, and our legacies, are the result of the million little choices we make throughout the day. Most without thinking.

If we were to pie-chart the way we spend our time, energy and attention, I think it's fair to say most of us would be shocked. Mortified might be a better word. And yet, we often have to be willing to get uncomfortable and real with ourselves before we can make any type of change.

So, what is that thing you've been meaning to do? That project you've been meaning to start? That program you've always wanted to launch? What is it that burns in your belly (and I'm not talking about the chili cheese fries you had for lunch), that you've never carved out the time to nurture and make happen? What is that big audacious dream that feels too enormous to even take a poke at? And how badly do you want it? Then ask yourself, what do I need to learn in order to make this happen, and what do I need to change in order to fit that in? (we'll unpack this further in the *Study Guide & Journal*).

While this topic may seem better suited for the Process section of the Penduka triad, possessing a student mindset is so foundational to realizing and developing our purpose that I had to put it here.

Our willingness to daily assume the role of student, intentionally feeding our areas of passion, broadening our knowledge base and cultivating our craft, directly affects the degree to which we will walk in our purpose.

If we are brave enough to examine our schedules and ask ourselves where our current time-spending habits will take us in a year, and where they could take us if we made some minor alterations, might we be motivated enough to change them?

• What if we committed to read for just 10 minutes each day? How might trading in that gossip magazine for a personal development, spiritual growth or business book each day effect your life?

• What if we committed to try our hand at a new craft - like painting or knitting - for half an hour every week?

• What if we used some of the time we mindlessly spend scrolling through social media to rather Youtube a new skill?

• What if we decided to listen to audio books, podcasts or a sermon while driving or folding laundry? What might we learn while doing mundane tasks we're already doing?

How different might your life look in a year?

Based on studies revealing the hundreds of hours and thousands of miles the average American spends in their automobiles every year, Zig Ziglar figured one could acquire the equivalent of a two-year degree in three years simply by listening to educational material in their car. He coined the term 'Automobile University'.

As I've mentioned before, I literally *Googled* and *Youtubed* my way through business. I have not taken one graphic design class in my life. Everything I learned in the first 6 years I gleaned from books, online tutorials and the occasional picking of someone's brain (this was long before I had business mentors or was a part of any entrepreneurial groups). By investing online time into something useful, rather than wasting it on celebrity status updates, my life looks very different than it did 9 years ago.

The ability we have today to learn new skills and to seek out excellent training in the comfort of our homes, astounds me. What would the brilliant minds of the past have to say about us having these top-notch educational resources at our fingertips...and then choosing mindless entertainment instead?

The bottom line is: what you feed grows, and where you focus your attention, your energy flows. Which begs the following questions...what are you feeding? Where are you spending your energy? And will you get a return on where you're investing your most limited resource; your precious time?

Are you intentionally developing and cultivating the gifts and talents God gave you, or are you wasting them? We have endless opportunities to grow and learn, but we have to choose to say no to mindless busyness and yes to actively pursuing growth.

"You have to apply yourself each day to becoming a little better. By becoming a little better each and every day, over a period of time, you will become a lot better."
John Wooden

DIG DEEPER ON PAGE 39
OF THE STUDY GUIDE

CHAPTER 14

E | EMBRACE FAILURE

*"Only those who dare
to fail greatly can
ever achieve greatly."*

ROBERT F. KENNEDY

Failure looms like the unknown beings in M. Night Shyamalan's movie, *The Village*. Bound by their fear of these mysterious creatures, described by the elders as "those we don't speak of", the youth vacillate between having to silence their ache for adventure and being paralyzed by their fear of the unknown.

We find out at the end of the movie - spoiler alert - that the elders have crafted a story to keep their village, nestled in the center of a game reserve, separate and untainted by outside influence. What held them captive existed only in their minds.

While we know in theory that most of the things we fear don't come to pass, there's something so terrifying about failure that it influences our decision making on a daily basis.

What is it about failure that terrifies us so?

Like we did with success, it's time to flip this subject over, prod its tender underbelly, and redefine this nebulous concept that strikes fear into even the bravest souls among us.

> *"Fear kills more dreams than failure ever will"*
> Dale Partridge

THE UP SIDE OF REGRET

I've started to sense a new feeling brewing in my belly over the past few years. Where a fear of failure used to rage, drowning out those whispers of longing and excitement, a regret-like feeling has surfaced. It isn't the ugly sort of regret that sits heavily on shoulders and furrows your brow, but more of a light grieving. A wondering as to what might have been had fear not held me hostage for all those years.

It shows up in random places. Like sporting events, or theater performances where stage makeup and feathered dresses make my heart race and my soul sing. How can a yearning so visceral have been silenced so completely? The ache to be a part of a team that trained together and played together. Why was I always too afraid to try out for the school play? To dance and sing and act?

Why did I allow so many years of my life to slip by in excruciating silence, all the while aching to belong to something big and colorful and vibrant?

I was completely and utterly paralyzed by fear. Fear of

not making the cut. Of failing extravagantly in front of a crowd. Or ending up as an unwanted addition to the team. Why risk failing, when you can just not try? Why risk the sting of rejection when it's easier to just *not* put yourself out there?

I carried that M.O. through high school and out into the world, through college classes, employment experiences and relationships. As long as I didn't try anything too brave and brazen, my fragile heart would stay intact.

What I didn't seem to recognize at the time, however, was that the reason failure wrecked me so, even in small doses, was because my heart had already been shredded. So hiding it didn't protect it, it simply allowed it to fester.

"Twenty years from now you will be more disappointed by the things that you didn't do than by the ones you did do. So throw off the bowlines. Sail away from the safe harbor. Catch the trade winds in your sails. Explore. Dream. Discover."
H. Jackson Brown Jr.

Maybe you didn't have a fierce aversion to looking like a fool in public, one that drove you out of the light and into hiding, but most of us can relate to fearing failure. And almost all of us can attest to being especially fond of our comfort zones.

But here's a reality check that may be hard to accept: a comfort zone may be comfortable, but nothing of substance grows there.

COMFORT ZONE KILLER

We all like being comfortable, I get it. That comfort zone of mine is warm, predictable and safe. Like the memory foam seats at the theater, it has the imprint of my derriere clearly imprinted in it. Apart from that dark corner where those little wounds quietly fester, it's just the way I like it. But comfort zones are for sleeping and brushing teeth and grocery shopping, not for dreaming and goal-crushing and world changing.

> When we realize that all the good stuff happens outside of our comfort zones, we may be less inclined to stay in them.

Even if you're not a "shoot for the moon" goal oriented personality, and just loving on your neighbor would be enough world-change for you (and it's an admirable aspiration) it still requires you to get out of your pajamas, leave your house and step on to someone else's turf. Or better yet, get over your hospitality-fears and invite them in. And that can be downright scary.

The truth is that comfort zones only give the illusion of safety and protection, because the only thing they keep us from is growth and freedom and authentic friendship.

When we spend our lives with risk-averse default settings, avoiding anything that could result in possible failure or rejection – while we might feel safe in the moment - we miss out on incredible opportunities to discover and learn and blossom.

Part of the problem with our aversion to failure is our short-sighted definitions of 'success' and 'failure'. As we discovered earlier on, they just aren't as black and white as we make them out to be.

We all know people who have succeeded wildly at something, and yet have ultimately failed at life. And then there are those who seem to have been predestined to fail, with all the makings of disaster woven into their DNA, who have risen above their circumstances and gone on to leave an indelible mark on society.

Some of the areas I've failed the most profoundly in have become areas I'm most passionate about helping others work through. Had it not been for my experience with "failure", and the things I learned in the process, I would have little hope and encouragement to offer.

Maybe it's time we redefine these words and start seeing failure for what it is: an opportunity to learn and grow.

"Failure should be our teacher, not our undertaker. Failure is delay, not defeat. It is a temporary detour, not a dead end. Failure is something we can avoid only by saying nothing, doing nothing, and being nothing."
Denis Waitley

THE BEAUTY OF RISK

The good news for newbie risk-takers is that it gets easier and easier to step out and take risks the more you do it. Maybe it is in discovering that we don't spontaneously combust after failing that we find courage growing in our bellies, or maybe it's simply a resilience that grows in the process of frequently risking failure and then embracing it when it comes. Or maybe it's both. Either way, when you tap into the wealth of wisdom piled up at the bottom of the proverbial success ladder, you'll notice all the fun you've been missing out on while staying buckled into your comfort zone. And by fun I mean wisdom, strength, resilience and courage. Oh, and adventure too.

When we realize that failure is not fatal, mistakes become incredible learning opportunities.

I have taken more creative business risks this past year than ever before, and while I've succeeded in some areas, I've failed stunningly in others. While I naturally love the thrill of succeeding, along with the momentum and energy it builds, I have learned more from my disasters and flops than I did on the gravy train.

When I mustered the courage to try my hand at designing and selling tee shirts for the police wives in my hubby's department, they sold like hotcakes. But when they started arriving from the printer, we were horrified to discover that the "Proud Blue Rose" ink was in fact a lovely shade of mint, and seeing none of our husbands lived the 'thin green line' life, I had a big mess on my hands. While tempted to throw in the towel, I learned a thing or two about the importance of bold communication and the use of Pantone color codes, scraped my pride off the sidewalk and pressed on.

When I got brave and flirted with my dream of running an online store, I sold 92 mugs in 48 hours. Then almost half of them broke in shipping. While my comfort zone called me, promising me endless days of unbroken mugs and unshattered pride, I pushed through. I learned how not to package and ship multiple breakable things, along with how to deal with postal insurance when they do break.

When I decided to try my hand at beading and metal stamping, I made several keychains for friends and family. Almost every one of them fell apart. Apparently not all metal jump rings are created equal. Go figure.

When a nasty review popped up on Amazon for my first book, I was devastated. Not only did their words hurt, but the fear of how others might respond to such a deeply personal piece of work made me wonder if I had what it took to live such a public life. While this wasn't a failure, per se, I had to process the fact that I had failed to please the masses. Which - while a ridiculous notion in the first place - still drives much of how we present ourselves and our creative work.

While I've always worn my heart on my sleeve, I've always played my cards close to my chest. Don't play the card, and you won't risk losing or getting laughed at. This was my motto and it served me well. Or so I thought. The problem with not extending your cards is that you don't play the game. I've sat on the sidelines, cards held close, for most of my life. And it breaks my heart to think of what that has cost me.

But friend...I've started to throw my cards in, and oh my goodness is it fun! Even when I realize, after the toss, that my card was in fact an UNO card and we're actually playing poker, I'm learning to laugh it off and find another card. The more you take risks, the easier it gets. I promise it does.

Fear of failure has loosened its death-grip on me and this is giving birth to freedom in almost every area of my life, from my relationships to my business endeavors. Where I used to be timid and self-conscious, I'm now just throwing ideas at the wall like spaghetti and seeing what sticks. And may I also say, the game of life is *way* more fun when you're actually playing in it rather than glumly watching from the sidelines.

> *"To live a creative life, we must lose*
> *our fear of being wrong"*
> Joseph Chilton Pearce

GETTING COMFORTABLE WITH BEING UNCOMFORTABLE

Stepping out of our comfort zones takes bravery, but staying out of our comfort zones takes boatloads of courage and resilience.

Maybe we need to "get comfortable with being uncomfortable". It's the line my kids most looked forward to in the Jillian Michaels workout DVD we used to do. They had heard it enough times that they knew when it was coming and could quote it to a tee. While my eyes shot daggers in her general direction when this phrase was uttered, now in surround sound, while I was trying to hold a less-than-comfortable pose, I was always thankful for the reminder that all the good things I'm working toward in life lie outside of my comfort zone.

The little protective bubbles we insulate ourselves with appear to minimize the risk of failure, but they cost us dearly. We remain stuck, faces pressed up against a glass ceiling, watching life happen around us. And that is not the life we were created for.

The past few years have been liberating ones for me in this department as I've started to care less about what people might think of me and how they might respond to my work, and have chosen rather to place value on pursuing those things that ignite my soul and spirit. Those things, after all, are why I believe I have breath in my lungs, and they can't survive within the confines of my comfort zone.

Like learning to embrace failure, the more comfortable we get with rejection – the less of a hold it will have on us. And the less of a hold it has on us, the more free and able we are to run hard after the things that really matter.

If you're a creative entrepreneur, you really have to get comfortable with rejection. Putting yourself out there, over and over again, is the only way to get your work out in front of people. If you don't bravely and strategically present your art, your writing, your speaking, your product...you'll have no customers. And with no customers, you cannot do this work you love. What feels so risky about the sharing of your work is that your work is an extension of you; it's the sweat from your brow and the blood from your veins, and when people don't respond, or they respond negatively, it cuts you to the quick. When our creativity is rejected, or ignored, it feels as though we have been rejected and ignored.

As tough as it is for me to swallow – as a self-professing,

recovering people-pleaser – I'm just not everybody's cup of tea. And it's okay. Really, it is. Not everyone will like what I create, say or write, and that's perfectly alright.

The more I dilute my message in an attempt to please the masses, the less of an impact my message will have on the ones it's intended for.

Bravery in this area not only cultivates confidence and creativity in business, but also creates a healthy environment for authentic friendship to grow, and vulnerability in marriage to thrive.

THE FEAR OF SUCCESS

Maybe you're conquering your fear of failure and have found, to your astonishment that you're now dealing with an unexpected case of fear of success. I've been confronted with those daunting 'what ifs' when stepping out into something new; "What if I can't keep up with the orders and make my customers mad?", "What if it grows so fast that I need to travel and leave my family more often?", and "What if this thing goes viral and then I realize I don't really want to do it?".

And beneath all of those anxiety producing 'what ifs' is the same troll who lurks beneath the other bridge: what if in all my success, I *fail in the end*.

"There is no comparison between that which is lost by not succeeding and that which is lost by not trying"
Francis Bacon

LEANING IN

Fear of failure is so tightly interwoven with a drive for perfection that sometimes it's hard to tell them apart. They seem to feed off of each other, intensifying the burden and the creative paralysis. While we'll uncover perfectionism for what it is in an upcoming chapter, it's important to recognize that the toxic cocktail of the two promptly can shut us up, and then shut us down.

This crippling fear is hugely to blame for our lack of action. And there's a nugget of smarts here - it is, after all, awfully hard to make a mistake while doing nothing. But it's also very hard to live a full, meaningful life while doing nothing.

Take a moment to close your eyes and breathe in slowly, then breathe out.

I'll wait.

If every breath in our lungs is measured by God, why are we so ridiculously fearful of stepping out? Do we really not trust that He'll come through for us each and every time? And that when He doesn't respond the way we hoped He would, that He then has something better in the works?

Risking failure is an exquisite opportunity to practice trust. So step out and risk it.
...Risk imperfection when it means completion.
...Risk rejection from the masses when it means honoring your authentic voice to the few.
...Risk getting your heart broken by allowing yourself to love someone again.
...Risk vulnerability when it means having a tough conversation with a friend.

...Risk failing at something grand so you can find your way to that something that's even grander.

Lean into it and allow yourself to feel what emerges in those moments. There are treasures to mine in failure that we won't find anywhere else. They teach us things about ourselves that we don't see while soaring to the top. They shape us and mold us in ways success and blanket acceptance never will.

Embracing failure helps us to master the art of bouncing back, as resilience is fostered through practice. This, of course, is far easier when you have your inner circle in place. This is where unconditional acceptance is needed, not from the masses, but from the few.

> "A life spent making mistakes is not only more honorable, but more useful than a life spent doing nothing"
> George Bernard Shaw

DIG DEEPER ON PAGE 41
OF THE STUDY GUIDE

In the next section we'll be taking PASSION and PURPOSE and turning them into action with the final segment, and the third leg of the Penduka stool; PROCESS.

"We don't have to engage in grand, heroic actions to participate in the process of change. Small acts, when multiplied by millions of people, can transform the world"

HOWARD ZINN

PROCESS

"It is not enough to be busy;
so are the ants. The questions is:
What are we busy about?"

HENRY DAVID THOREAU

If passion is the fuel that drives us, and purpose the why that directs the journey, then process is quite simply the mode of travel. It harnesses the power of focus and momentum, and the wise, intentional stewarding of time, energy and talent.

Think of the first two components as the motion-activated hand dryer on a bathroom wall. It's wired and ready, full of hot, explosive potential...just waiting for you to step up and move your hands beneath it. Passion and purpose, dynamic and exciting as they are, require action to be of any consequence. And this is where the fleshing out of process comes into play.

When our passion and our purpose collide with a productive process, magic happens. It's simply impossible for it *not* to happen when these three forces are working together.

The beauty of the process is that it confirms and amplifies our passions and purpose through action because they're almost always easier to identify and call out when we're actually moving.

I initially wanted to entitle this section 'produce', based on the concept of productivity, but was concerned that this battle cry might do more harm than good. Because it's not just about producing results, it's about being effective. Fruitfulness will always be more valuable than busyness. It's also less likely to result in cardiac arrest, which is always a bonus.

It's not about doing more things faster. It is about doing the right things well.

This section is going to require you to put some skin in the game. You see, the hardest part isn't knowing what to do, it's doing something with what you already know.

In this information age, it's easy to be glutted with knowledge. What sets the movers and the shakers apart from everyone else is that they take what they've learned and they do something with it.

In other words, knowledge is useless without action.

Shocked as you might be to learn this, you'll never learn how to skydive by reading books and listening to podcasts. You can love medical shows and study neurology for years, but if there's been no practical application or action, step away from my head with that scalpel. While those information gathering practices are good, you have got to put what you know into action. Action is a game changer. It's what separates the dreamers from the doers.

We are all busy. Drowning in an age where overflowing schedules are glorified and busyness is a badge of honor, the question we need to ask ourselves is, are we busy doing the right things? Are we using our precious, limited time to accomplish the stuff that matters the most?

Let's rock the joint!

"The secret of getting ahead
is getting started"
Mark Twain

CHAPTER 15

P | PROTECT YOUR YES

"Do what you feel in your
heart to be right – for
you'll be criticized anyway"

ELEANOR ROOSEVELT

Where do you consider the wealthiest place on earth to be? The diamond mines of South Africa or maybe the oil fields of Saudi Arabia? What about the thriving economy of Monaco which, with its big yachts and fast cars now rates[20] above Norway, Switzerland and Qatar?

Les Brown and Myles Monroe have both been quoted as declaring the cemetery as the wealthiest spot on earth. Not because of heirloom rings on the fingers of rich old ladies buried there or heaps of gold that kings insisted be buried with their corpses, but because of the astounding amount of untapped potential that lies there.

BURIED AND UNBORN

Buried beneath the dirt lie song lyrics that were never recorded, masterpieces that were never painted, books that were never penned, non-profits that were never started, and projects that weren't launched. Here lie inventions that were never created, programs that were not initiated, buildings that were not built and medicine that was never formulated.

In those burial plots lie ideas that were never birthed and dreams that never came to fruition, and we're left to wonder why. Why on earth did these people take these ground-breaking, world-shaking, culture-shaping things to the grave with them?

Were they fiercely insecure? Fearful of what others might say if they dared to share publicly what was percolating internally? Was it that all-too-familiar concern that if they put themselves out there, they might be criticized, laughed at, or even rejected?

Was it the risk of failure that kept them silent, and unfulfilled?

Did they stop just short of success? Did they try and fail and try and fail enough times that they threw in the towel prematurely? Had they tried just one more time, or just one more way, might they have changed the world with their ideas?

While I'm certain there's a myriad of reasons why these creations remain uncreated and these dreams lie unrealized, I have to wonder how many of these tragic souls were just too busy doing other things to spend time doing the right things.

In a society where the glorification of busy is alive and well, it's not a hard proposition to entertain. Were these people too wrapped up in the never-ending 'urgent' list to check things off the 'important' list?

Maybe in the chaos of life some lost themselves to numbing agents like drugs and alcohol, and in their attempt to drown out their pain, they silenced their creativity as well.

Less obvious in its dream-delaying power, and yet equally as potent, is the compulsion to say yes to every good thing. But if it's good, you might ask, isn't it exactly the thing we should be filling our days with? Well, no, it really isn't. If I were to hazard a guess, it would be this very thing that sends people to their grave still full of unrealized dreams.

*"I will not die an unlived life.
I will not live in fear of falling or catching fire.
I choose to inhabit my days,
to allow my living to open me,
to make me less afraid, more accessible;
to loosen my heart until it becomes a wing,
a torch, a promise.
I choose to risk my significance,
To live so that which came to me as seed
goes to the next as blossom,
and that which came to me as blossom,
goes on as fruit."*
Dawna Markova

WHY GOOD IS THE ENEMY

I love good things. Good food, good people, good habits, good movies, good shoes, good ol' fashioned face-to-face conversation over a good cup of tea. Good is good, right? Well, yes. And no. When it comes to spending our lives and choosing what to fill our days with, good can mean the death of great things.

While I'm not usually a very black-and-white gal - I tend to live my life in the many shades of grace between the two - when it comes to my daily routines and habits, I am. I mentally compartmentalize things into two main categories; good and bad. And this is where it gets tricky.

We could literally pack our days with good things; good meetings with good people, good organizations that need us to volunteer our time and our talent, good committees that would like our input and participation and good charities that need our money. We can collaborate with several good businesses that are on the verge of launching yet another good thing, and we can mentor every one of those 13 good people who asked to meet for coffee next week. We can contribute to those good websites looking for good content, and commit to that good friend who just asked us to take that good exercise class 3 nights a week. If we think for a moment that this would lead to a mighty good life, we're dead wrong.

Every action has a consequence in the same way we reap what we sow. But whether it's a helpful, life-giving consequence or a destructive, soul-sucking one depends on what we sow. And what we say yes to.

There are so many good things we could fill our days with that I wonder how many well-intentioned people lie on their deathbed wondering what on earth happened. If their lives were filled to the brim with good things, why did that lingering sense of emptiness and lack of fulfillment persist? I believe it's because we do not more carefully steward our "yes".

STEWARDING OUR YES

We forget that we are a limited resource. There is only so much of us to go around. We've gained a basic understanding of our time and energy being limited, but our most valuable asset - ourselves - is the most limited thing around and we so often neglect to protect it.

Every time we say "yes" to something or someone, we are saying "no" to something or someone else. Every *yes* comes with an equally weighty *no*.

The devastating realization that I'm sure many have as they reflect back on their busy lives is that they said yes to so many "good" things that they didn't have the time or energy to say *yes* to what truly mattered. To the best things.

As Jim Collins puts it, *"good is the enemy of great"*.

The concept of protecting your *yes* is harder to grasp if you're a people-pleaser. I don't like to disappoint people, and I especially don't like letting people down if there's a risk they won't like me because of it. If you're a person of authority in my life (read: influential leader), there's even more of an obligation to keep you happy. Although spelling it out like this makes me wonder why I've wasted so much time living life this way. It's quite ridiculous really.

As an RPP (recovering people-pleaser), this is something I've intentionally been working on for some time now. During one of my counseling sessions with Carol, she brought up the subject of boundaries. I have a feeling the subject arose upon her sudden realization of my complete lack thereof. I kid you not, I literally sat back in my chair, envisioned little dotted lines forming a circle around an aerial view of myself and said, "Oh yes...those. I completely forgot about boundaries!".

REBUILDING THE WALLS

Despite having read the book[21] years before, I had totally neglected to see how broken down and, let's be honest, non-existent, my boundaries had become. I had allowed other people to shape my days by not having the guts to say *no* to them. They were all up in my space because I had allowed it, and I'd functioned that way for so long that I couldn't even see it.

Coming away from that counseling session lit a fire in me to rebuild and protect my boundaries. I started looking at my schedule through a different lens and realized that the only person I had to blame for the weary place I found myself in was me. Out of fear of disappointing people I had said yes to so many things - all good things - that I had little time and energy to say yes to the best things. To the people and projects that mattered most to me. And this book was one of them.

As I sit here typing this, it's 6:15am on January 1st, 2016. I'm exhausted from ringing in the new year with my wee ones, and fighting a headache from all those final pieces of chocolate I crammed in before giving it up for the new year. But I'm here. And I'm only here because I made a commitment to myself that starting today I would rise daily at 5am until this book was finished. It is something I've chosen to say yes to this year.

As I said earlier, every *yes* comes with a *no*. This isn't optional and you can't outsmart it. If you don't intentionally choose what you say *yes* and *no* to, the default response will be issued and you may not like it, or even realize it, until it's too late.

I said *yes* to enough other things last year that I inadvertently said *no* to writing. In order to finish this book this year, more specifically this month, I've had to say no to other things. To ensure the right things make it into my schedule and the wrong things stay out - "good" as they might be - I've made my intentions clear. I'm fiercely protecting my time for the next 3 months by not taking on any new projects, speaking engagements, or graphic design and coaching clients.

> By clearly spelling out what I'm saying *yes* to, it has become far easier to swiftly and kindly say to *no* to others. We don't have to make excuses, we can simply be gracious and firm with our *no*.

When we deliberately say *no* to the constant, unrelenting demands of the world (social media, email, news, etc.), we're free to say *yes* to living fully in the moment; to impromptu dance parties in the kitchen when Uptown Funk blasts through the speakers, and to whispered requests of "Mommy, can you hold me for a minute?". All the other stuff is negotiable.

Protecting our yes and stewarding our time and talent as the precious resources they are will greatly increase the likelihood that we will skid into home base fully spent, totally empty, leaving no untapped treasures behind in the grave.

"It's only by saying "no" that you can concentrate on the things that are really important"

Steve Jobs

DIG DEEPER ON PAGE 45
OF THE STUDY GUIDE

CHAPTER 16

R | REPEAT IT & REAP

"We become what
we repeatedly do"

SEAN COVEY

I heard a story of a young woman who was taking on the responsibility of preparing the annual Christmas ham for the first time. It was somewhat of an intimidating task as this spectacular chunk of meat was the talk of the town. It was always beautifully moist and glazed to perfection. This year it was her turn to pull off the meal that had been handed down through generations of domestically savvy women. As she stood in her kitchen in front of the meat, she decided to call on her mom's experience.

"Mom, how exactly do I do this ham thing?".

"Oh, it's really not that complicated, honey...you just need to make sure you follow the steps". She listened as her mother paused to scroll through her mental recipe book in search of the secret sauce. "You preheat the oven to 350°, cut the ham in half, and then prepare the glaze while the oven heats up. It's all about the maraschino cherries and cloves, dear".

As the mother rattled off the ingredients and measurements, the young woman inquired, "Why do I cut it in half first?".

"Well...I guess I'm not sure, dear, my mother always did. It must have something to do with more surface area to caramelize? I guess I've never thought to ask. Just follow the steps".

Being the inquisitive millennial she was, she called her grandmother after hanging up with her mom. "Grandma, talk to be about this ham...". Hearing the steps again, as if experiencing her previous conversation on repeat, she decided to go one step further.

Freshly nestled into an assisted living home, her great-grandmother was seldom far from the phone. "Can you tell me about your famous ham, grammy? Why do you cut it in half first?".

Laughing, the matriarch whispered, "Because I never had a roasting pan large enough to hold the whole thing, dear!".

How easily we go through the motions, doing things we've always done because, well...we've always done them.

> *"If you always do what you've always done,*
> *you'll always get what you've always got."*
> Henry Ford

THE GOOD NEWS ABOUT HABITS

We've all heard it; "practice makes perfect". It was used in an attempt to lessen my loathing for practicing scales and arpeggios as a six-year-old. It was jokingly said in reference to intimacy in marriage during the early years. And I've heard it said in regard to good business practice.

But the truth is, practice does not make perfect, it makes permanent. Which begs the question...what is it we're practicing exactly? In the way we use our time, energy and resources? What has become our default setting simply by way of repetition?

If our lives and legacies are made up of a million little things we do, often in mindless repetition, it makes sense to pause and ask ourselves what we're doing, and more importantly, why we're doing it.

> Our small daily habits matter more than any big fancy thing we may occasionally accomplish. And it's the consistency with which we do them that packs the punch.

The bad news is: most of the frustration, disappointment and lack of progress you experience is your responsibility.

The good news is: most of the frustration, disappointment and lack of progress you experience is your responsibility.

Nobody can live our lives for us, so no one can change and shape and mold our lives the way we can. We are fully responsible for our lives; the choices we make, the relationships we foster, the way in which we spend our time, the foods we eat, the entertainment we select, and the way in which we respond to the things that are outside of our control. And this truly is good news!

We have more authority and are more powerful than we

realize, and until we acknowledge these truths, we won't step into the fullness of the life we were created for.

"If you want something you've never had, you must be willing to do something you've never done"
Thomas Jefferson

While we tend to make small commitments to big change, our minds and bodies respond better to big commitments to small changes.

Let me explain it this way...

What if instead of big change (think New Year's resolutions and lofty goals) with little commitment (no system or plan of attack), we started making a big commitment (I'm going to do this for 30 days, no backing out) to make a small change (I will do 20 squats each morning when I'm brushing my teeth).

When we acknowledge the power of small, daily habits to change the course of our lives, we harness the power of what Darren Hardy calls the *"Compound Effect*[22]*"* and Jeff Olsen refers to as the *"Slight Edge*[23]*"*. It's the small, seemingly insignificant things, repeated every single day, that have enormous positive - or negative - effects on our lives.

Consider these small actions and the negative effects they have:

• I will start smoking tomorrow, but will only have one cigarette each day

• I will express my frustration with my spouse more often, but will only call them one bad name each day

• I will sleep just 10 minutes longer each morning, and arrive just a few minutes late to work each day

• I will stop at the drive-thru for a burger just once each day. And make the coke a diet.

- I will check my phone every five minutes, but only to see if I need to respond to anyone.

- Immediately upon waking, I will mull over 3 negative things people said to me the day before

- I will watch just one more episode of my favorite TV show each night and get less sleep at night

Sounds ludicrous, doesn't it. But do you see how small actions that become daily habits have a huge impact on our attitudes, in our relationships, and on our overall health?

As silly as that list may read, this stuff thrills me to pieces. It's mind-blowing, really. Because if small negative habits done daily can reap such devastating effects, imagine how small positive habits done daily can transform one's life!

What if you implemented these small actions into your daily life for 30 days:

- I will drink one glass of water immediately when I rise in the morning

- I will express one thing I appreciate about my spouse every day with a genuine smile and eye contact

- I will hug and squeeze each one of my children for 10 seconds every day

- I will eat one colorful salad every day

- I will set my alarm for 5 minutes earlier than usual and read one Proverb each day

- I will read 10 pages of a personal-development book every day before bed

- I will set a timer for 15 minutes and do simple exercises until it goes off

These small things, repeated daily, will make a big difference.

"The people you surround yourself with influence your behaviors, so choose friends who have healthy habits."
Dan Buettner

A THOUSAND LITTLE CHOICES

Our very lives, and legacies, are the result of the thousands of little choices we make throughout the day. Often without thinking.

A fascinating thing about habits, and the way we tend to manage them, is that our natural inclination is to weed out the bad habits first. And while there's wisdom in kicking a bad habit as quickly as humanly possible, there can be such an overwhelming sense of defeat from previous failed attempts that we start the endeavor already feeling defeated.

Rather than focusing on the bad habits you want to get rid of, choosing to focus on the good habits you want to implement can build momentum and produce faster results.

While we only have two children, laundry is my nemesis. It seems that while I'm still basking in the honeyglow of getting it all sorted and put away, the mountain of dirty clothes is taking over the laundry room again. I seem to tackle them in loads of 4, when my husband starts noticing the obvious lack of clean underwear in his drawer. Part of the problem is my bad habit of using the trunk at the foot of our bed as a clothes hamper. The pile grows and grows until I finally throw it all in the laundry, or find I have the equivalent of a fifth basket to put away. My hubby and I recently committed to making our bed every day. It never ceases to amaze me how the simple act of making my bed motivates me to keep my trunk clear and clothes put away, which inspires me to keep the laundry heap under control. Every time I walk back to my room, throughout the day, I smile at how beautifully clean and organized my space is.

As you change one small thing for the positive, you'll reap the benefits of the action, which will propel you to make more small positive changes in your day. Isn't it interesting how choosing the salad at lunch, despite the fact that the smothered burger sounded crazily amazing, affects other decisions throughout your day? I know that when I'm eating well, it inspires me to move more, and when I'm exercising more, it motivates me to eat better.

Every little act that lines up with your greater goals of living a life of passion and purpose (and organization and health are key to making this happen) compounds to build energy and momentum, inspiring other simple acts and wise decisions. Who knew the simple act of making one's bed could have such a profound ripple effect on the day?

As you focus more on implementing good habits than removing the bad, the good will naturally create less room for the bad, or better yet, you'll lose your appetite for them altogether.

And by "bad" I mean anything that doesn't feed your soul and spirit, doesn't line up with your core values, and doesn't fuel your life's mission. So yes, bad is a broad, sweeping word and covers everything from drinking excessively and picking your nose to eating too many Big Macs and spending hours mindlessly scrolling through social media.

You know your vice and you know what it does to you.

Or maybe you don't and you need a reminder of how fruitful and beautiful life can be without it. Maybe a little dramatic for a nose-picker, but you get the point.

Much like foods can have the similar caloric value but carry startlingly different nutritional profiles, small substitutes in bite-sized time-chunks can make a big difference:

• 15 minutes spent reading a professional development book will always have greater impact on your future than an hour spent reading a gossip magazine.
• 15 minutes spent reading the Bible will do far more for your emotional and spiritual health than an hour spent comparing yourself to others on Instagram.
• 15 minutes spent doing a series of squats, lunges and push-up will do greater things for your energy levels than another hour spent in bed after hitting the snooze button for the third time.

The small things matter, and they always have. They make up the often unnoticed rudder that steers the ship of our lives.

THE POWER OF ROUTINE

In the same way brushing your teeth before bed isn't something you have to will yourself to do (although, there have been nights...), it's just a habit. We've done it for long enough that it doesn't take thought. It's a non-negotiable, if you will.

When we introduce small, but pivotal, habits into our lives as non-negotiables that we're going to determinately choose to do for long enough to make it a habit - they become a part of how we do life.

When I committed to rising at 5am every morning to write until this book was completed, I was both excited and terrified. I am not a morning person by nature. I quite happily stay awake until all hours of the morning, via the midnight avenue, and would be happy as a lark sleeping until 9am every morning. I have a favorite pillow, a signature left-laying fetal position (pillow tucked between knees) and sleep like a baby until the very last minute possible. I love my sleep. So committing to rise at 5am each morning was no small feat.

But as much as I love sleep, I love a good challenge even more. Having also cut out refined sugar from my diet, I am officially running on caffeine, willpower and grace, thankyouverymuch.

But here I sit, just before 6am, having done my 'writing morning' routine. Josh Groban sings to me sweetly at 5am, I'm drinking water over the kitchen sink with one eye open by 5:03. I pop the kettle on and then pop a squat against the wall. It's a good way to squeeze in a little exercise and get my blood pumping. Between the boil and the 5 minutes it takes to brew my first cup of tea, I squat against a wall and read the *First 5* devotional on my phone. I resist the urge to dip into the black hole of Facebook or Instagram until I've written for at least an hour.

I'm sitting in my writing chair by 5:15, having checked the woodstove, fed the cat, and pried my second eye open. Because this isn't something I have to think about each morning - "do I really want to get up and write at 5am?" - it just happens. It's a non-negotiable. I don't have to think about it or wrestle with myself about whether to get up or hit the snooze button. Or reset the alarm altogether. I just do it because it's become a routine. Alarm goes off, I get up. There's no room for deliberation anymore.

Admittedly, there are days I sit and stare at my screen like a zombie for 27 minutes before moving any one of my fingers, but hey, all is grace, right?

When the first weekend of the year came around and school had started up again, the sweetness of sleeping in on a Saturday started to woo me. I had a decision to make; sleep in until 8 for two days and enjoy a whirlwind affair with my pillow, or keep up with the early mornings. While I knew I'd enjoy sleeping in on those mornings, I also knew it would cost me. It would mean having to drag through my Mondays and Tuesdays due to having thrown off my rhythm completely.

I'm a go-big-or-go-home kind of girl, and thrive off of routine and consistency. My body and my head need it. So I settled on sleeping until 5:30am on weekends, which my night-owl self balks at, but my get-things-done personality loves because there's still an element of 'dessert' in there that sets the weekend apart.

The greatest benefit, however, is that I'm not punishing myself in the long run by messing with a routine. We are creatures of habit, and when we mess with the habit, we mess with the outcome and ultimately with its success.

Consistency is huge when it comes to setting yourself up to succeed. This applies to my relationship with sugar too. I'm either in, or I'm out. I just don't do moderation.

When we realize how instrumental simple positive practices are in our daily lives, we won't want to return to our previous way of doing things.

SENSITIVITY AND GRACE

Two quick things I want to add as side notes before we wrap this chapter up.

Firstly, it's really important to note here how very differently we're wired. What motivates one person may not motivate another. One method might inspire incredible results from one, and render another paralyzed and overwhelmed. Rather than compare and resent our differences, it's important that we acknowledge them and honor them. Be sensitive to your body, listen to your internal dialog and monitor your physical responses, and then do what works best for you, because what works best for you is something you're more likely to stick to.

Next, a quick note to mommas with wee babes. It is nearly impossible to be consistent when your children's routines are anything but. Their sleep patterns are often unpredictable, germs mess with the best laid plans, and tears have a way of throwing off everything else you're trying to do. I get it. Being consistent with habits, while raising children, is a bust. But don't give up. Give yourself an extraordinary amount of grace, be flexible, and don't stop trying. This is a season and a new normal will come. You're doing the best work you can possibly do right now, fashioning arrows you will one day shoot out into the world, and the greatest habit you can practice right now is resting in God's sufficiency to carry you through even the poopiest of days.

"We are what we repeatedly do.
Excellence, then, is not an act, but a habit."
Aristotle

DIG DEEPER ON PAGE 47
OF THE STUDY GUIDE

CHAPTER 17

O | OPEN UP SPACE

"When a man is wrapped
up in himself, he makes
a pretty small package"

JOHN RUSKIN

I have a confession to make. I'm that woman who is so set on not having two random dirty dishes in the sink, or 3 rogue shirts left in the laundry basket, that I load the machines to capacity. Okay, maybe a little beyond capacity. Fine. A lottle.

When it's packed full and I find more things, I simply find creative ways to insert them in cracks and crevices - in the name of having an empty sink or basket. It's a bad habit disguised as a good one. What do you make of that?

I'm also the woman who has the husband who then remarks, "Umm, this shirt still stinks like an armpit" or "Why is there food remnant crusted on this plate?".

I know. It's disgusting. And maybe it's my sneaky attempt to weasel my way out of these chores, but here's the thing: when we stuff our cycles to capacity, nothing comes out clean.

If we don't allow space for refreshment to flow and create room for movement to happen, we'll discover the unmistakable smell of exhaustion along with the shrapnel of ground up relationship on the surface of our souls.

FINDING HEART IN THE HUSTLE

Can we just take a moment to talk about hustle? Because *enough* already.

I have a love-hate relationship with this word. I love the energy it carries in female entrepreneurial circles and the way it ignites passion and laser-focus when emblazoned in gold on cute white mugs drunk out of by women with red lipstick and messy buns. It has a pretty fabulous image, really. I mean, 'hashtag hustle', right?

I love its call to action. In a day and age when all the best information is right at our fingertips and it would be easy as pie to become glutted on knowledge, action calls us to more and is ultimately what sets the dreamers apart from the doers. Hustle invites us to make.things.happen. Boom!

But here's where my love affair with the word dies a sudden death. Hustle doesn't know when to quit.

I loathe the never ending high-impact, low-grade scurry it

seems to imply. Always going, always striving, always pumping out #allthethings. There is just no room for white space in hustle.

In a culture that demands constant activity and is up to its eyeballs in hustle, I struggle with the perpetual idolization of busyness. It starts in elementary school and doesn't slow down. We learn at a young age to become human doings instead of human beings. That our value is somehow linked to what we accomplish and in how short a time.

I don't just want to be busy, I want to be fruitful. I don't just want to do more things faster, I want to do the right things well. I don't want to teach my kids that keeping up with the Jones's extracurricular activities is what makes life worth living, or family dinners worth missing.

As Lysa Terkuerst so eloquently put it in her book *The Best Yes*[24], we cannot afford to live life "with the stress of an overwhelmed schedule" or we will ache "with the sadness of an underwhelmed soul".

Is your heart health a priority? And I don't just mean that glorious lump of cardiovascular muscle that rhythmically pumps blood through your veins. I'm talking about you. Your soul, your mind, your emotions. Are you carving out time to be quiet, without distraction, for even 5 minutes? And no, locking the bathroom door and lingering a little longer on the pot does not count.

Are you creating space to play? To paint or bake or stretch. To laugh. Are you taking care of you?

> *"The most regretful people on earth are those who felt the call to creative work, who felt their own creative power restive and uprising, and gave to it neither power nor time."*
> *Mary Oliver*

In a world that demands our attention at every turn, are you slowing down enough to notice the roses, not to mention smell them?

Are you creating and capitalizing on the small pockets of time throughout your day to nourish yourself by feeding your soul and spirit? Because here's what you need to realize. If you don't, it won't happen. No one else can do it for you.

> The health of your soul is your responsibility and cannot be palmed off on someone else. Which means we cannot blame others when we're weary or overwhelmed. This is both a hefty responsibility and a liberating truth.

You are in charge of you, and it's up to you to protect your most valuable asset; you.

Think of this as the oxygen mask spiel on an airplane. You have to take care of yourself first. As selfish as this feels and sounds, especially when we're commissioned to put others before ourselves[25], by prioritizing self-care we're able to take care of others. I have little of value to extend to you if I don't first protect and nurture my own heart, health and emotions. I may be able to do extravagant exploits for you, for a while, but I will soon crash and burn if I haven't first secured my own mask.

We simply cannot give away what we do not have.

WELCOMING WHITE SPACE

Have you ever wondered why you get hit with creative inspiration when you're driving alone on open road or when you're in the shower? If you're a momma with small children, please notice the emphasis on the word *alone*. Driving with crying or arguing children inspires a lot of things, but I'm pretty sure 'creative' is not the word we'd use to describe it.

The reason we get struck with brilliance in these two unusual spots - and why I always have the voice-recorder app open on my phone and an eyeliner in the shower for 'wall notes' when I'm working on a big project - is because we're doing a task that requires physical engagement, though usually on autopilot, while our heads are free to be creative.

This white space - free from the clutter of multitasking, where our attention and energy are spread thin between tasks - provides ample space for our minds and imaginations to play.

> Waking your soul up - and keeping it engaged
> in what truly matters - requires scheduling
> open space into your life.

This requires us to learn one of the most powerful words in the English language, "no", and use it often. Only when we have margin - in our schedules, our bank accounts and our energy stores - can we intentionally say "yes" with open hearts and open homes to those around us.

As we take care of ourselves, we're fueled and focused to then turn outward to encourage and love on others.

Can I be painfully honest for a moment? This might feel a little uncomfortable for a while, but hear me out. I'm a little concerned about something.

Like all new phases and popular crazes, blogging and social media movements brought with them splendid opportunities as well as slippery slopes. We have, at our very fingertips, the opportunity to connect with people all over the world in real time. This alone is mind-blowing. We have the ability to gather into tribes with like-minded women who can inspire, encourage and equip each other in different fields. We now have the capacity to run legitimate businesses with beautiful websites and top-notch products from our homes, while wearing pajamas and sipping tea, sporting red lips and messy buns.

But we also have the opportunity to get sucked into an online world where we can network with a bajillion fabulous people, and miss out on the life that's happening all around us. In the flesh. Truthy and unfiltered.

In our addiction to the mindless scroll, we miss many of the moments that matter most. And it's understandable. The photo-shopped, beautifully lit, filtered squares of perfection that fill our feeds are far prettier than real life, with its funky smells, dirty dishes and awkward humans.

We love to be liked and applauded and celebrated. And with the instant approval we're able to acquire from fans and followers, and the ease with which we can shut out the nasty ones, it's easy to understand why we get sucked into the thrill of online businesses and blogs and brands. We can control our hub of happy, revealing as much or as little as we wish, then simply step out of it when we're done.

It's easy to build walls and guard our vulnerable places when closure means simply clicking a button. But we weren't called to build walls. Boundaries, oh heck yes. But walls, no.

So what about those people who live next door?   And that family down the road who just moved into town? And that strange kid who keeps calling you mom and asking for more food?

What about those very real people in your community who pose a very real threat to your nicely erected walls. Will we let them into our messy imperfect homes to experience our messy imperfect lives? And if we muster the courage, do we have enough white space in our schedules to make this happen? Because if we don't, there's a problem.

And herein lies my concern. What are we missing in our addiction to hustle? What are we neglecting on the homefront in favor of cultivating an online following?

> If we want to make a difference in this world, it starts with making a difference in our local community.

We have no place trying to change the world out there if we can't first love the people right in front of our faces. We don't have to abandon the former to nurture the latter, but we have got to get our priorities straight. And we need space to do it.

"We must use time wisely and forever realize that the time is always ripe to do right"
Nelson Mandela

THE ART OF NEIGHBORING

In the same way that prioritizing your marriage is vital to the health of your family, prioritizing the people in your immediate circle of influence enables you to authentically ripple out impact to a wider circle. Often organically and indirectly. And it all boils down to stewardship.

Maybe you think of finances when you hear the term 'stewardship', but it is simply defined as the planning and managing of our resources. This includes your time, your talents and your energy. While finances are renewable and your talents evolve and grow, your energy and time do not. I know we've tackled these subjects at length already, but I wanted to look at them again through the lens of local community.

I often read about movers and shakers who are lauded online as thought leaders and world changers, and I wonder, "What would the lonely single neighbor three houses down say about them?". "What would the janitor at their kid's school have to say?". Are they as present and engaged on their home base as they are in the larger community where they can selectively put their best foot forward and only engage when it's convenient for them?

I realize that this may come across as unkind or even judgmental, but my intention is to offer a friendly word of caution. As important as hustle and accomplishment are on the global scale, local presence and in-the-flesh community is more so. As important as saying yes to exciting online opportunities may be, saying yes to the people God's placed in your neighborhood is more so.

You've been called to bloom where you're planted, passionately, purposefully and generously. While it's an attractive notion to want to send out our vines into the world and sprout pretty blossoms all over the place, where likes and heart-eye emojis are prolific, I believe we first have a responsibility to the community we're in.

And with no open space in our schedules, we will find we have no open space in our hearts.

We take the charge to "love your neighbor" seriously. We believe God actually meant that we were to invest in our community and pour into our neighborhood. We believe in the power of simply opening up our home and the beauty of breaking bread together, even if the chicken is dry and the carpet is unvacuumed. This will not happen by accident in the five minute pockets of breathing room between activities, or if we're not intentional about unplugging our minds from the web.

We will forever be reluctant to embrace real, messy life

when air-brushed perfection becomes the standard by which we measure it. And the way we measure life will directly influence the way we go about living it.

> *"A healthy social life is found only, when in the mirror of each soul the whole community finds its reflection, and when in the whole community the virtue of each one is living"*
> Rudolf Steiner

DIG DEEPER ON PAGE 49
OF THE STUDY GUIDE

CHAPTER 18

C | CRASH THE COMPARTMENTS

"To accomplish great
things, we must not only act,
but also dream; not only
plan, but also believe"

ANATOLE FRANCE

Even if you're not a particularly organized person, we tend to like to organize into compartments the way we think about our lives.

There's a cloud shaped box filled with hopes and dreams and unbelievable amounts of childlike creativity, and there's a room filled with the weight of reality, piles of paper and bills. There's a box for education and one for entertainment. The latter is often bigger than the former.

There's an emotions wing, filled with compartments a plenty. The 'love we feel for our friends and family' section, and the 'how we feel about politicians' room. The 'how we talk to people we respect' department is in the loft, while the 'things we say to ourselves' corner is in the basement. There's the happy box and the sad box and an anxious box and, lest we forget, the angry box. This one has a red hue.

There's a box for Monday through Friday, where we eek out all the mindless keep-showing-up-for-a-paycheck, and press-through-the-school-week stuff. A more enjoyable section for Saturdays, and then a somewhat ominous religion box we keep for sacred things. Like Sundays. And guilt. And funerals. For many, this is where God lives.

There's the health box, where thoughts like 'I should eat more kale' and 'but Burger King sounds so good' wrestle on the rug. We visit this box when we're reminded of our mortality. Right after we stop by the religion box. We stop in more often around the first of the year and after birthdays. Or when friends get scary diagnoses.

There's the somewhat exhausting 'for public consumption' box and the 'nobody gets to see this level of crazy' box. Women literally take up residence in that box once a month.

While often hard to define, our minds are filled with box upon box inside rooms within wings where we label and file away thoughts and feelings regarding different topics. It's the epitome of organized chaos and it's enough to drive us absolutely batty.

COMPARTMENTALIZED

Three of the largest compartments we identify are mind, body and spirit. We section off and divide what we feel goes into the three different categories and tend to them individually. If there's a problem in one of the boxes, we shift our attention to it and attempt to sort through the chaos by rearranging the things we've stuffed in there. Sometimes we relabel its contents, add a new habit or toss out an old one.

The divisions we assume exist between the three realms seem convenient enough, offering a level of insulation to each. When we're struggling with our physical health, feeling sluggish and unmotivated to take care of our bodies, we want to be able to close that box and move it to the side so we can focus on what is working *for* us.

If a dry season in our spiritual journey has led us away from communion with God, it's convenient to be able to brush it off as the fluffy ethereal element of our lives and get on with it.

Or if we're struggling with unforgiveness toward someone, and it's manifesting in bouts of depression and anger, we can wrap up the box extra prettily, slap a bow on it and just pretend that all is well with our souls.

But that's not how it works.

Because here's the thing about those boxes. While we may see them and try to manage them individually - maybe we even find some sort of comfort in being able to contain and control them - they don't exist independently. Nope. They don't. There are literally no neat dividers that separate all that body stuff from the mental, emotional and spiritual stuff.

They are all intricately connected and woven together. When there's a lack of health in one area, it affects all three. Without fail.

When God breathed life into your being and declared it time to make your grand entrance on planet earth - in all your slimy, squirmy glory - you, my friend, were a package deal.

When we neglect our mental health, which falls into the 'soul' category along with our emotions and will, it leaks over into our physical and spiritual health and wreaks havoc. Revisit the 'Ask Questions' chapter if you're in need of a reminder of just how directly our thoughts and feelings impact our physical reality.

So feed your mind wisely.

Because our spiritual lives cannot be contained in a shiny little Sunday box, try as we might to make it conform, our willingness to engage in and cultivate our spiritual health trickles over into the way we think and feel about ourselves and others, even showing up in our countenance. Remember that as palpable as our fleshy bodies are, they will one day fade away. While it's a concept we struggle to wrap our heads around; our spirits are eternal and are far more real than our bodies. What happens in the spiritual realm, because it's at the center of who we are, drives everything else and determines the final outcome.

So feed your spirit wisely.

Add to these powerful connections the impact our diet has on our overall well-being, and you've got yourself the most elaborate single-thread tapestry ever made. What we put in our bodies - where our gut is referred to by some scientists as "our second brain" - has a direct effect on the clarity of our thoughts, our energy levels, and our mood.

So feed your body wisely.

As exquisitely designed, integrated human beings with spirit, mind and body intertwined, we need to approach our lives from a more holistic understanding, working to cultivate health within the whole, to experience the fullness of life for which we were created.

Over twenty-five-hundred years ago a Greek philosopher advised that we "ought not to attempt to cure the eyes without the head, or the head without the body...the body without the soul. For the part can never be well unless the whole is well." Plato nailed it.

I think it's fair to say the vast majority of us know exactly what we should – and shouldn't - be doing, and yet continue on in our destructive ways. We devastate our souls by ingesting hordes of trashy media, we neglect our bodies in favor of highly-processed "food-like" substances, and we neglect our spirits in order to squeeze in extra sleep or a little more hustle.

Our physical health effects our emotional health, which effects our spiritual health, which effects our physical health and our emotional health, which...well, you get the point.

What we put in our mouths, what we allow to take root in our spirits, and what we neglect to filter from our minds directly impacts how well we function as an integrated human being and whether we fulfill our purpose with our passion intact.

"The body becomes the battlefield for the war games of our mind. All the unresolved thoughts and emotions, the negativity we hold on to, show up in the body and makes us sick"
Brian Seward, PhD

What would it take for us to realize how ridiculously valuable, and incredibly vulnerable, our bodies are? And how essential their whole health is to our ability to flesh out our calling.

I guarantee you, no matter how old and decrepit the car in your driveway might be, you know what it takes to run - and run well. Mountain Dew and donuts would destroy it because it requires a specific fuel to function. As do we! Your body is the vehicle in which you navigate this life, and last time I checked, there were no backups. How we choose to fuel our bodies makes all the difference in the world! And how much more valuable we are than a rusty old jalopy (or even a sexy new Mustang).

I desperately want to steward this one life I've been given to the best of my ability, and I simply cannot do it with a sick, fatigued body, an anxious heart and an unstable mind.

On the flip-side of that, can you imagine the joy of living with all these areas aligned and healthy!

CHOOSING LIFE

According to legend, tribal hunters wanting to catch monkeys would nail a coconut to the trunk of a tree and drill a hole just large enough for a monkey's little hand to slip in. Inserting a ripe banana into the coconut, they would lie in wait for their prey. Soon enough a monkey would come along, reach in, grab the banana and – with his tightly-clenched fist stuck inside the coconut – await his fate.

All the monkey had to do to escape and be free was let go of the banana and slip out its hand. Fist tightly wrapped around a would-be last meal, the short-sighted, impulsive nature of the monkey demanded its banana at the expense of its life.

So my friend, I want to ask you...what soggy, coconut-scented banana are you clinging to? What counterfeit are you settling for that now has you stuck? What do you need to let go of that is holding you captive to a less-than-abundant, fruitful life?

Wellness is not a vain pursuit. It literally means the difference between surviving and thriving. And we were made to thrive.

Think about it. We were created to accomplish extraordinary things through simple acts of ordinary stewardship - just showing up, day after day after day, to love and lead and serve and grow - but when our health is diminished, so is our impact and influence.

When we intentionally choose to feed our spirits, inspire our minds and revive our bodies we create a powerful synergy that enables us to experience the fullness of the life we were created for. And it's out of this vibrant, effervescent place that our lives can have the greatest impact.

"Use your health, even to the point of wearing it out. That is what it is for. Spend all you have before you die; do not outlive yourself."
George Bernard Shaw

DIG DEEPER ON PAGE 51
OF THE STUDY GUIDE

CHAPTER 19

E | EXIT HERE, PERFECTION

"Perfectionism is a twenty-ton
shield that we lug around thinking
it will protect us when, in fact,
it's the thing that's really
preventing us from taking flight".

BRENE BROWN

"That's perfect!". I didn't realize how often those seemingly harmless words slipped from my lips in everyday parenting moments until it started to show up in her. She was 3 the first time it smacked me in the face.

She had worked on her coloring project for twenty minutes - which in 3-year-old time, assuming it works somewhat like cat years, is the equivalent of about two hours in adult time - and had placed it up on the counter next to me.

I had been chopping veggies for dinner when out of the corner of my eye I noticed it. After putting it down, she brought her little arm back up and, fanning her fingers widely on her artwork, brought her nose up to the edge of the surface and carefully swiveled it until it fitted perfectly in the corner of the kitchen counter. It wasn't enough that she had created a masterpiece and delivered it to me, it needed to sit squarely within the constraints of the countertop corner...approximately half an inch in from both edges. She corrected it because the way she had presented it wasn't perfect.

I'm pretty sure my throat closed up as I realized what had just happened. She pulled a "Joy". And recognizing this inspired the opposite in me.

Parenting has a way of bringing all your controlling, perfectionistic tendencies to the surface, along with every other less than delightful quality you may possess. There's something about rearing 30 pounds of fiercely independent, insanely stubborn human that exposes them. You're wise to pick your battles. And you're *kind* to them when you do whatever it takes to protect them from the condition that cripples so many of us: perfectionism.

Even if we wouldn't describe ourselves as perfectionists, we're all susceptible to the influence of media and pop culture.

We're reminded constantly what beautiful looks like, intelligent sounds like, successful feels like and sexy behaves like. There's a distinct mold that try as we might, we don't fit in.

Even when we manage to pull off a great show, we know when the curtain falls and the stage lights go out, that the mask must come off too.

> *"The thing that is really hard, and really amazing,*
> *is giving up on being perfect and beginning*
> *the work of becoming yourself."*
> Anna Quindlen

PERFECTION IS THE ENEMY

As a raging perfectionist, this has been a beast to conquer. In fact, it's a battle I still have to fight daily to keep it in check. Perfectionism is like a single drop of dye that quietly works its way through every ounce of life, starting in one corner and permeating the whole. I've seen the effects of it color everything from my marriage and mothering to my house keeping and work.

It's like a dollop of dog poo in a batch of brownies; undercover but unmistakable. Comparatively small yet strangely overpowering.

The possibility of delivering imperfect work will cripple your small business in the same way fear of never having a perfect home will destroy your social life: you won't bravely put stuff out there and you won't bravely let people in.

The knowledge of how childbirth permanently transformed the skin you're in, placing you even further from perfection than before, robs you of confidence with your spouse and keeps you covered up and distant.

The additional danger in comparing ourselves to some airbrushed version of perfect is that our daughters are watching. They know how hard we work to present the best version of ourselves with ideal lighting, angles and filters. They're more perceptive than we give them credit for. They see the way we look at our bodies in the mirror and pine for our frizzy hair to get its act together. They hear the way we talk about our weight and how we berate our misplaced curves and imperfect skin, and they start to use our measuring stick to measure themselves.

We will never measure up to what society deems ideal and the sooner we realize we don't have to - and broadcast this liberating truth to our daughters - the sooner we'll embrace our perfectly imperfect selves.

Perfection is critical when it comes to bridges and airplane wings, but it's over-rated in almost every other area of life. Don't get me wrong, as a graphic designer I believe there is a place for perfection, but there's an even bigger space for *excellence*.

When perfection becomes the standard by which you measure everything, you spend your days exhausted, hyper-critical and anxious. Feeling both out of control and never quite enough.

I cannot tell you how many posts I haven't written, projects I haven't completed, designs I haven't shared, and talks I haven't developed because of my inability to get them "perfect" enough for public consumption.

I would be willing to bet that I'm not alone in the stuffing down and snuffing out of imperfect offerings. Could perfectionism be another reason people quietly drag their unshared treasures into the grave with them?

While a busyness and fear of failure are often to blame for lack of action, perfectionism - and the procrastination it feeds

- might just be one of the biggest culprits.

ENTER MOMENTUM

Perfectionists are especially skilled in over-thinking and under-acting. The reality is that holding ourselves to this unattainable standard of perfection will cripple our ability to act, which will in turn disable our ability to capitalize on the power of momentum.

Contrary to popular belief, action isn't inspired by passion. While a powerful cocktail of passion and conviction make for a good catalyst, passion alone is not reliable enough to keep us going. Action is necessary to fuel the fire and activate the principles of momentum.

> *"It is never the size of your problem that*
> *is the problem. It's a lack of momentum."*
> John C. Maxwell

Picture yourself on a big swing. You're not moving, and the chains seem to reach forever into the sky. It is going to take work to get this thing going. Whether you choose to lean back and start pumping your legs like a mad woman, or you take a few steps back and hike yourself up as high as possible on your tippy-toes, getting moving requires action.

Action is always the first step, and you should know, perfectionism will always delay action.

As you start moving, excitement builds (or maybe it's nausea) and pumping shifts into high gear. As passion grows, the work gets easier and pumping more fluid. By the time you're flying high, the combination of work and excitement make keeping the swing in motion as easy as leaning into the movement.

In other words,

$$passion + action = momentum \rightarrow more\ passion$$
$$passion + perfectionism = paralysis \rightarrow less\ passion$$

If you recall Newton's First Law of motion from high-school physics, you'll remember the "Law of Inertia"; objects at rest tend to stay at rest, unless activated, and objects in motion tend to stay in motion, unless their momentum is stopped. As Darren Hardy so delightfully puts it, "Couch potatoes tend to stay couch potatoes, while achievers - people who get into a successful rhythm - continue busting their butts and end up achieving more and more".

Note that action has to come first, whether you feel the passion or not. You see, passion is more a result of action, than the cause of it.

Once you're physically engaged in the process, you've created space for passion to grow and develop, spurring on more action, and then out of the blue, momentum shows up to the party.

We've seen this play out in marriages many times as we've mentored couples over the years. One or both of the spouses isn't feeling anything. They don't want to engage emotionally or physically with the other. There is no passion and they take that lack of passion as a reason to prove that there's nothing there. It doesn't measure up to the perfect image of marital bliss they had in their minds, and so they stay stuck.

But as we challenge them to take action first, regardless of what they feel like doing, passion usually follows. Eventually momentum grows as action and passion continue to play off of each other, creating a dance of work and grace.

Maybe that's where the phrase "fake it till you make it" comes from. Show up and keep showing up, and something is bound to happen. But if you wait for everything to be perfect before you act, nothing will ever change. This applies to relationships, developing healthy habits in eating and exercise, deepening your spiritual walk, and to pursuing the work you were created to do.

The law of momentum is the honored guest at the party, but it waits patiently for you to courageously and imperfectly act before it shows up with another bottle of passion to be uncorked.

Referred to as "Big Mo" in his book, *The 21 Irrefutable Laws of Leadership*[26], John Maxwell notes that momentum not only magnifies success, but has a way of minimizing problems and obstacles. He points out that it energizes and motivates, is easier to steer than to start, and is a powerful change agent. He wraps this up by stating that it's also very much our responsibility.

While building and experiencing momentum is exciting, it's directly linked to action, and with action comes the risk of error. This is where the recovering perfectionist gets to fight the temptation to hyperventilate and choose rather to claim "progress over perfection" as their new mantra.

While perfection cripples, progress inspires.
Where perfection paralyzes, progress completes.

As Emily Ley[27] declares, "I will hold myself to a standard of grace not perfection".

*"We learn to walk by falling, to talk by babbling,
to shoot a basket by missing, and to color the inside
of a square by scribbling outside the box."*
Tal Ben-Shahar

Aren't you thankful that our profound ability to err is part of what makes us human? Mistakes happen when you're moving. It's why pencils come with erasers. We all make mistakes and we all need opportunities for a do-over.

The beauty of momentum is that it is far easier to course correct when you're in motion, than when you're stationary. Try turning the steering wheel of a parked car if you're not sure what I'm talking about.

BREAKING UP WITH PERFECTION

In a nutshell, just do it.

Trade in perfection for excellence, and cling to grace in the process. Sometimes our courageous unpolished action will result in a mess we have to clean up, but we have to refuse to allow that to extinguish our momentum. A completed yet imperfect offering will always have more of an impact on the world than something never perfected enough to even be offered.

If we're content to do our best - rather than be the best - we'll discover a joy and freedom in our lives that would have quickly been incinerated by the kiln of perfectionism.

Do that thing you need to do, without the need for a pleasure factor and without the need for it to be perfect, and the ripple effect will be enormous. Allow your brave action to build passion, to create momentum and to give birth to a new life-giving rhythm or grace.

Your marriage, your health, your vocation, and your soul will benefit because of it, and your purpose will be beautifully evident in the process.

"A life spent making mistakes is not only more honorable, but more useful than a life spent doing nothing"
George Bernard Shaw

DIG DEEPER ON PAGE 56
OF THE STUDY GUIDE

CHAPTER 20

S | STOP SWITCHTASKING

"Juggling is an illusion.
In reality, the balls are
being independently caught
and thrown in rapid succession.
It is actually task switching."

GARY KELLER

Shortly after we moved out into the country, where well water is the norm, we had a softener put in and a reverse osmosis (RO) tank installed beneath the sink. While we only use the RO water for drinking and cooking, it gets its fair share of action throughout the day.

The problem with this little water spigot that pivots just to the right of the sink, is that the flow isn't nearly as fast as the main faucet so it takes longer to fill things up.

This is cause for concern for a passionate (read: impatient) tea drinker when the hankering hits, for one must satisfy the craving as soon as humanly possible. We drink British blend with milk and the occasional drizzle of honey, in case you're wondering. I've been drinking it since I was a wee tyke, when my parents started giving a weak version of it to us girls in baby bottles.

It remains my drug of choice and I unashamedly blame my addiction on them. But I digress.

I fill up the kettle for tea anywhere between 3 to 127 times a day. But standing there holding the kettle under the spigot until it fills up is excruciating. There are so many other things I could be doing with those 42 seconds. So I put the kettle on the counter right next to the sink, pivot the spout and flip the RO switch on. Then I head off, grabbing things out of the fridge, wiping down the counter, letting the cat back inside. And more than a handful of times, I've become distracted by small tasks and started on another, until I'm interrupted by a curious splashing sound coming from the kitchen. It's then that I remember the kettle and run, only to find purified water flooding the counter and floor in front of the sink. I've done it, my hubby has done it, and our kiddos have also done it while filling up mason jars for dinner time.

One would think that having done this before, more than once, I would have learned my lesson, but no. I have become such a chronic multitasker that I simply cannot stand there and wait while it fills up. My compulsion to accomplish things in small bursts has driven me to a level of distractibility that is unprecedented. I've got issues, people.

After flooding the kitchen by way of the RO system, for the fifth time, we noticed that there was some movement in the ceramic tiles we'd laid down in the kitchen a couple of years before. Eventually after one of them cracked in two, we pulled it up to find the mortar mushy and the cement board beneath it soaked. Slowly but surely the grout cracked and today we have a section of about 7 tiles that still need to be pulled up, scraped out and reinstalled.

Needless to say, the slightest sound of trickle from anywhere in the house, makes me move like a ninja cat on speed to the kitchen sink. It strikes horror into my bones.

In an attempt to prevent further tile damage, my hubby instituted a rule that 'one's hand may not be removed from the vessel being filled while the RO is on'. Loosely interpreted to mean: if you do not remain glued to the sink until all water transfer is complete, no candy for the next month.

I try to honor this rule as much as possible, really I do, but often I get the urge to make tea when I'm in the middle of something. This means I'm going into the act already preoccupied, which greatly increases the likelihood of said rule being broken, and the floor getting a spontaneous washing. But shhh, don't tell him.

Just yesterday I was filling the kettle, being a good girl and 'hovering' until the task was completed. Mentally wrapped up in the project I was working on, I flipped the lever, left the kettle there and walked away to finish the project. To my utter horror, I heard the signature drip-drip-drip that precedes the gushing of water onto the already destroyed tile floor. Running through, I discovered I'd been so wrapped up in what I was doing that I hadn't flipped the RO lever off, I had mindlessly flipped the little switch on the kettle that turns it on when it's on its base, and had left the water flowing.

Oh girl, I have problems. I may need a 12 step program.

We women know how to get things done, and we've mastered the art of doing #allthethings. All at the same time. If you're a mom, you probably feel you have a PhD in Multitasking. It's sort of a required skill to keep children alive.

But here's the thing...it isn't actually a thing.

I'm sorry to have to break it to you this way, but multitasking isn't actually a thing. It isn't. It's a persistent myth and a destructive habit we keep trying to perfect in the name of getting more things done. I may have the ability to do several things at once, but if I'm honest...none of them is done well. Hence my astonishing ability to burn pancakes, flood the kitchen, email the wrong thing to the wrong person, and deliver hollow responses to my children's thoughtful questions. In one fell swoop.

While this multitasking truth may initially come as a shock to you, I think you may find this section liberating.

"Multi-tasking is great in the kitchen when you are trying to time the chicken to be ready at the same time as the potatoes. But do not assume it is a great way to manage a workday."
Joanne Tombrakos

THE MYTH OF MULTITASKING

A word we've been using to describe our to-do-list crushing prowess was first used in 1965 by IBM in a report[28] that described their new computers ability to run several programs concurrently. But back then, before technology boasted multiple processors in a single unit (which allow us to simultaneously stream music while typing an email), it simply meant that the computer now had the ability to have multiple programs open in the background, switching quickly between them as you opened and worked in each one.

In essence, what we've coined 'multitasking' is more accurately described as 'switchtasking'. In much the same way the original computers could run numerous things in the background, we can watch television, page through a magazine and eat, or walk and talk at the same time. And much like they could only have one program active in the forefront at a one time, we can only give our full attention to one thing at a time.

It is neurologically impossible for the human brain to actively focus on more than one thing at a time, but we have mastered the distracted art of switching quickly and almost compulsively from one project to another. We are masters of the switch-task. The problem with this way of functioning is that as the number of things we try to juggle at one time increases, our ability to do them with any level of competence decreases.

We have become a society who simply cannot focus on one thing for any length of time.

We've all experienced 'mindless eating', finding ourselves standing before an open fridge in a foraging haze for the 3rd time in fifteen minutes. And we're not even hungry. We've experienced the remote hog, most often our fathers or our husbands, who sat on the couch channel surfing, watching everything and yet, watching nothing.

Today we practice the infamous 'mindless scroll'. We reach for our smart phones, without so much as an alert to suggest we do so, and find our thumb doing its signature up-downward-drag maneuver. We seem to have developed a compulsive need to check our phones every 3.2 seconds, sucking our already distracted minds into more mindless activity more often than we'd care to admit.

Whether your kryptonite is social media, email, the news, or the contents of your fridge, numerous studies[29] have revealed that we now check things mindlessly out of habit, rather than need.

As someone who thrives off what's new and exciting, this became a real problem for me during my work day. I would open several projects, in an effort to not forget them, and would switch between them throughout the day. The moment I got bored with what I was doing, I'd remember another project I had to work on and switch my focus. "Ooooh, shiny!", I would think, running off to play with a new design, research for talk prep, or wrap up new orders. Switching again a little bit later to something else I'd committed to finish. Back and forth, here and there, attention scattered and spread thin.

I refer to this as 'barracuda syndrome'; I'm distracted by the next sparkly thing on my to-do list (and several that weren't, but had caught my eye). Even if my hands don't follow my mind, once my mind has moved onto something else, I've lost momentum.

As a creative soul, this is especially hard. I thrive off of fresh inspiration, adore the challenge of learning a new skill, and see entrepreneurial potential everywhere. I love starting new things, but once the initial sparkle has dulled, it takes incredible discipline to follow through because there's always an exciting new opportunity flirting with me from afar.

I seem to have a constant flow of ideas backed up in the creative pipeline, and it takes every ounce of restraint to not want to stick my finger in every.single.one. I could paint signs! Or I could create jewelry! I want to make pallet art...no, string art! Oh, I could create art with pebbles. I think I want to try spoken word poetry. I should start a Youtube channel. Oooh, I could decorate cookies and sell them in pretty packages. No, wait! I could write Bible studies and start a podcast. #allthefreakingthings. It's both exhilarating and exhausting to live inside my head.

OUR OBSESSION

And can I just get real up here for a moment? Being a

creative gal is just one of the excuses I have for being scatterbrained and all over the place. The truth is, I seek out affirmation and validation from outside sources, like a junkie hunting down their next fix. Or like we search out the last box of chocolate-covered Oreos when our emotions are running ragged and we're seeking instant comfort.

Whether your crack is Instagram, Facebook, or your blog comments, it's incredibly easy to get sucked into a cycle of approval addiction - for the rush of endorphins we enjoy when we're 'approved of' – only to find that it requires another hit. And another.

But what about when we don't find what we're looking for? And no one has liked or followed or applauded what you're doing? Now not only are we distracted, but we feel defeated, and that is even more damaging to the process than switchtasking.

This constant need to see what others are doing, or rather what they think about what we're doing, is driving us to chronically distracted living. We're signed into everything except that which matters most; our marriages, our parenting, our creative process, and even into our spiritual lives.

We see it every time we go out to eat. Couples or families staring at their phones, switchtasking their way through dinner, social media and each other. We all know who comes up short.

I feel it pulling me when I'm at the park with my kids. "I wonder if anyone responded to my post yet...I can finally watch that new watercolor tutorial...I could read that awesome article on hedgehogs". Something. Because just sitting on a park bench in the sunshine enjoying watching my kids is apparently no longer enough.

I feel it pulling at the basketball game. "I wonder if my client responded and whether we're going ahead with this big project. I bet I could peek really fast and no one would notice". And the next thing I know, people are cheering because my son scored the winning basket and I was checking my email.

I see it seeping into my marriage where it's especially hurtful to a 'quality time[30]' husband who craves my undivided attention and will not get it unless I unplug from everything else.

And I find that when I grasp onto these things that promise to deliver what only real life can, these counterfeit lovers latch on and suck life out. It takes careful, intentional discipline to weed the need for them out of our lives.

And let me just say, when I choose to stay engaged in the moment, focusing on one profoundly simple thing - being present - there is a ridiculous amount of peace, love and contentment to be found there. And when I intentionally avoid social media as a quick fix for this approval addiction - which tends to empty me rather than fill me - I remember that I'm already approved of by the only One who truly matters.

> *"We have to get back to the beauty*
> *of just being alive in this present moment"*
> *Mary McDonnell*

YOUR ONE THING

A constant switching of focus and tasks throughout my work day were resulting in me feeling exhausted by the end of it, without enjoying a sense of accomplishment. I was always busy and yet decidedly unproductive.

Part of the problem was my severe case of 'barracuda syndrome', while a good portion of it was due to my inability to say no - which I'm learning to correct by fiercely protecting my yes.

Juggling several projects at once became such a common practice for me that I struggled to stay engaged in one for long. Call it creative avoidance, call it chronic distraction, all I know is I was tired of treading water and going nowhere.

Maybe you can relate?

Whether it's in hobby, home or work, our promotion of multitasking and celebration of busyness has crippled our ability to focus on one thing at a time... and finish it well.

I recently finished two excellent books that tackled this problem head on. Essentialism[31] and The One Thing[32] both expose the myth of multitasking and urge us to focus on fewer things with more intention, and challenge us to change the way in which we plan and go about our days. I would highly recommend them to anyone who struggles with focus and follow-through due to trying to manage too many things at once.

What blew me away - and convinced me that I could no longer afford to switchtask - were the statistics. Each time we shift our focus from one thing to another, we lose productivity by 40%[33], while it takes an average of 20 minutes[34] to re-engage at the original level of work before the distraction, and often by then, we've moved onto something else. Or been sucked into Facebook again.

If you can imagine an echocardiogram, that squiggly line would represent our attention span - our ability to focus and do our best work - when we're allowing ourselves to shift from one thing to the next.

While this is still a struggle for me, I have found that cutting my day up into chunks has helped tremendously. I'll map out my ideal week, creating flexible time-blocks for email, design, writing, coaching, talk prep, product creation and order fulfillment. When meetings, speaking engagements or appointments have me out of the studio, I rework my week based on what needs to get done first. By allowing myself chunks of time to focus fully on something without distraction (I turn off email alerts and close social media), I build momentum and accomplish far more than I did before. And in far less time.

The feeling of accomplishment that comes with following through and finishing something, propels me into my next time block with fresh energy and focus for the next thing. Scheduling time to check my email helps me stay in control of my day, rather than my day being controlled by my inbox.

Setting a timer for social media check-ins also helps me not participate in the mindless scroll that swallows precious time and tends to leave me stuck in the comparison trap.

Breaking my day, my week, my months and my year loosely into chunks (like the three months I set aside to focus on this book), allows me to focus on what's important and play off the momentum that builds as I buckle down and make things happen. It also makes it easier to say 'no' to things that don't line up with my big picture 'yes'.

If our daily habits create our weekly realities, which form our busy months that make up our jam-packed year, it's not hard to see how our ability to pare back and focus on fruitfulness will guide our journey to purpose.

"Concentrate all your thoughts upon the work at hand. The sun's rays do not burn until brought to a focus."
Alexander Graham Bell

DIG DEEPER ON PAGE 59
OF THE STUDY GUIDE

CHAPTER 21

S | START SMALL

"Patience and the
passing of time do more
than strength and fury"

JEAN DE LA FONTAINE

When we first moved out into the country several years ago, we decided that some more trees and bushes were in order for our almost 4 acres. We started researching and shopping around for what might flourish best in our area and what would serve as pretty fillers without being high maintenance (because a gardener, I am not). I soon spotted forsythia in what seemed like every other yard and started drooling over the gorgeous sprays of yellow blooms.

Our hunt ended when we received a packet in the mail from the Arbor Day Foundation offering us an incredible deal on shrubs, bushes and trees. We went to town ordering crabapples, lilacs, sugar maples, a hawthorn, and a couple of forsythia.

I was giddy at the thought of what would soon arrive on our doorstep. At the sound of every squealing truck brake, I checked the driveway for the FEDEX guy. I could practically smell the scent of Spring blossoms lingering in the air. Those majestic sprays of gold and gorgeous sprigs of pink would soon fill the open spaces of our yard, and every mason jar in our house.

I'm sure you can imagine how baffled I was when a cardboard tube arrived in the mail from the Arbor Day Foundation. What an unusual way to ship planting and maintenance information.

Surely they could have simply attached tags to the trees when they arrived on the truck?

My jaw literally dropped when inside the tube we discovered 10 color-coded sticks.   Bam, our order had arrived!

Apparently these were the 10 trees we had ordered, each marked with a unique color to specify their kind. You have got to be kidding me, I thought. These were not the lovely plants we were expecting. These were quite literally twigs with roots.

My visions of spring arrangements peppered with long, leggy sprigs of yellow and pink died a sudden death.

After the initial disappointment wore off, a sense of foolishness started to settle in. Did I honestly think I could score a mature bush or tree for $3.99, no matter how desperately I willed it to be so?

But I had expected it, and I continue to expect it - wisdom and growth, on the cheap - only to be awkwardly reminded that it only occurs over time, and at a high price.

We didn't see much growth those first two years.   Not because they weren't growing, but because all of the growth was happening beneath the surface, where anchoring and establishment needed to take place first. As we unearthed in the 'Inspect Your Roots' chapter, for us to grow and thrive up and out we must first tend to our roots as they reach down and into.

It's been 4 years since we planted those, um...sticks...and while the maples have been mowed over and the crabapple is just tickling our knees, the forsythia is well over our heads and is in desperate need of a trim.

In a world that applauds big and bold and flashy, and tends to ignore small and simple and seemingly insignificant, it's easy to adopt this method of measurement in our own lives.

THE EXPECTATION GAP

Not only do we ache to be noticed, we resent the smallness of our lives. We see where we want to be, but are painfully aware of where we are.

Todd Henry[35] describes the journey as a "U". We start excited and hopeful, and can see our destination on the next hilltop right from the hilltop we're standing on. Our gaze is locked, a path is mapped and we're excited to conquer the hill. But as we venture down the trail and into the valley, our view of our destination is limited and we get discouraged. The woods are scary, especially in the dark, and we wonder if we're cut out for this.

This wild 'U' shape we travel can throw even the most adventurous traveler off, but is all a part of the journey.

The uncomfortable space between what we expect and what we're experiencing is where we spend most of our lives.

It's the dash that will one day be inscribed on our tombstone and is really the only thing we have any control over. This expectation gap can be a place of bitterness and exhaustion, or of growth and maturity. We can either foster resentment, or we can posture our hearts to celebrate the purpose - and yes, even the pain - in the process.

I love the story my mom tells of a famous sculptor who was asked by someone who'd stopped to admire his work, how it was that he was able to so beautifully extract a statue of a horse from a block of marble. The sculptor smiled and responded, "Why, it's easy! I simply look at it from this angle, and from that angle...and then again from this angle, and finally I just chip away everything that's not horse."

The chipping away of the excess that currently covers up who we are is a slow process, but we can trust the One who holds the chisel. You and I are in the process of waking up to who we were created to be, and the treasure isn't just what awaits us at the end, it's in what is being undertaken along the way.

"Wherever you are, be all there"
Jim Elliot

CELEBRATING SMALL

Life isn't an A to Z leap. It's an A to B step, and a B to C shuffle. It's a C to E hop, with a little back-to-D moment before we revisit the E. Sometimes we hobble and sometimes we crawl, but as long as we keep moving forward we're exactly where we need to be. While we'd love to hurtle right to Z, our purpose is what passionately gets fleshed out in the in-between.

It seems natural to celebrate the big things in life; the wins, the successes, and the moments we accomplish great things.

But when these are the moments we live for, and strive for, we miss out on the beauty and significance of the everyday. And life is what happens in the small moments.

While our lives may feature several epic moments to throw parties over, when we learn to notice and value the small things, we'll discover moments worth celebrating every day.

...The little wins, like choosing the baby carrots over the Doritos. Again.

...The times your eyes catch your husband's and the two of you linger just a little longer in the moment.

...The daily showing up and being brave, even just for the one conversation you've been avoiding for a month.

...The choice to kneel down and whisper parenting correction instead of bellowing from on high.

...Starting that book you've always wanted to write, even if it was only the title you wrote down.

...Catching yourself before saying something negative to yourself in the mirror. And smiling instead.

...The sacrifice you made of 10 minutes of sleep to get up and read your Bible.

...Deciding to turn the TV off and go for a walk instead.

...Reading that ridiculous book for the 28th time because that little one in your lap won't always be that little.

While I'm a naturally positive person, I'm also incredibly hard on myself. I focus my energy on perfecting all the kinks in the system, and tend to dwell on the areas I fall short. Add to this disastrous habit my tendency to look at all the amazing things others are accomplishing and then glance back at the messy stuff I'm hashing through. Now I realize you may be thinking, "What?! You wrote this book...you're supposed to have this stuff down". I don't. It's true what they say, we write and speak from the pit of our own struggle.

These destructive patterns were not only sapping my joy,

but were developing a toxic level of dissatisfaction in my soul. I found I was going to sleep with a pervasive heaviness in my heart, and during a particularly low season last year, God confronted it.

"Joy, you are profoundly accomplished at obsessing over your weaknesses. Now I want you to funnel all of that energy into celebrating your strengths, small as they may be at times, and to focus on all that is right in your world". Boom!

I had become so caught up in the comparison trap, allowing my drive for perfection to suck the life out of the journey, and He was inviting me to slow down, step back, and celebrate the small things.

In an effort to foster a greater sense of purpose within the smallness, I pulled out one of my many journals and started to list 3 simple things each day. Little moments to celebrate, minor accomplishments and brave unspoken paradigm shifts. Sometimes it was as simple as "I chose to play checkers with the kids today...when I didn't want to" or "I took the time to just sit with someone who needed encouragement today". Or "I'm still writing in this silly journal".

As I remind my little loin-fruit frequently, "Look for the bad, and you'll find it. Look for the good, and you'll find it!". You'll find what you're looking for, sweet friend, and when you start looking for signs of growth, hard as they may be to spot at first, and then pausing to celebrate the heck out of them, you'll find a year from now, you'll look back and treasure those thousand small steps you made.

These are the things we need to throw dance parties in kitchens for. Because this is where change begins and habits form. It's the simple putting of one foot in front of the other, celebrating the wins and rebounding quickly from the losses.

Choosing to focus on the positive and actively looking for the good in each day, we'll *do* this.

> *"Do not despise these small beginnings,*
> *for the Lord rejoices to see the work begin..."*
> Zechariah 4:10

Whether you live the life you were created to live, or hobble along in survival mode, boils down to two things; the choices you make and the disciplines you employ in the small, seemingly-insignificant moments of life.

You've got this, friend. We've got this. We were created for greatness and we have everything we need to accomplish our calling already hardwired into us in seed form. We just need to call it out, nurture it, protect it and be brave with it.

It's not about 'go big or go home'. It's about courageously showing up - day after day after ordinary day - and embracing this beautiful, messy journey. We have got to learn to be faithful in the ordinary things on ordinary days. Because it's in this consistent showing up and being present in the everyday smallness of it all that leads to an extraordinary life.

It's here that we truly discover what we've been created for.

God is in the process of building an altar of His goodness and grace with our lives, and He doesn't use one giant slab of stone. He uses millions of small pebbles, one after the other, moment after moment over the course of our lives, and beyond as the ripple effect of legacy continues.

We desperately want our lives to accomplish their purpose, but there's always a process to fulfilling the promise. And it's in the process that our passion is ignited and our purpose discovered and fulfilled.

"You can achieve anything you want in life if you have the courage to dream it, the intelligence to make a realistic plan, and the will to see that plan through to the end."

Sidney A. Friedman

DIG DEEPER ON PAGE 61
OF THE STUDY GUIDE

FINAL THOUGHTS

"We must be careful with our lives,
for Christ's sake, because it would
seem that they are the only lives
we are going to have in this puzzling
and perilous world, and so they are
very precious and what we do
with them matters enormously."

FREDERICK BUECHNER

What is the point of being alive if we're not going to at least try to create something extraordinary with our lives?

I feel the need to warn you that when you tap into purpose and ignite your passion, be prepared to face opposition. While I hesitate to get all super-spiritual on you, you need to know you have an enemy. Once your soul is awake and your spirit alive, you pose a tremendous threat to his plans[36]. If there's one thing our enemy hates, it's women who have woken up to their calling and chartered the course to flesh it out. It makes you dangerous, and *that* makes you a target.

Take heart, dear one, when you're feeling under attack. This enemy isn't threatened by souls fast asleep. Thieves, after all, only focus their attention on high-value treasures.

When you realize that your passion has purpose and that you've been strategically placed and equipped right where you are, your whole outlook on life will change. Nothing will be arbitrary.

You will lead courageously and live creatively and love lavishly because you'll understand the value you bring to the table. You will embrace radical faith and brave vulnerability, and know that in the small ordinary moments, extraordinary things are taking place.

You'll discover that retirement isn't an option because your calling doesn't end until your last breath has been taken.

You will die *empty*, having lived *fully*; scuffed knees, dirt beneath your nails, having collected memories rather than dreams, having given of yourself the very thing you were born to deliver.

You will have lived the life you were created for.

So live.

Dismantle your inner snooze button and turn the light on. Arise and shine, sweet one. It's time to *wake up*.

> *"...I urge you to live a life worthy of the
> calling you have received."*
> Ephesians 4:1b

"Don't ask what
the world needs.
Ask what makes
you come alive,
and go do it.
Because what the
world needs is people
who have come alive"

HOWARD THURMAN

ACKNOWLEDGMENTS
My humble gratitude goes out to:

Joe, my sweet man; without your support and encouragement this book would never have emerged. Not only have you freed me up to write and create, but you've offered insight and wisdom along the way. You have my undying gratitude for the constant flow of hot beverages and grace you provided while this project emerged. Thank you for asking me to marry you (especially the second time). I will love you forever.

Mom, you are extraordinary. The selfless way in which you pour yourself out for others both inspires and challenges me. You feed not only mouths, but weary souls and hungry spirits. Thank you for believing in me when I didn't believe in myself, and for showing me what it looks like to love Jesus wholeheartedly in the everyday.

To my sisters; you three rock my face off! God totally knew what He was doing when He squeezed all four of us into one family. Your wisdom, talent, generosity, authenticity and, lest I forget, your wicked senses of humor, make you the coolest sisters a gal could have in the history of ever.

And to the women who have walked with me over the years, pouring life and love into my soul and drawing out the gold I often forgot was there. You are my people; the mentors, spiritual moms, warriors, confidants, comrades, and companions God has blessed me with on this journey, and I am who I am because of you:
Christine L., Gwennie J., Corinne M. & Cindra F. | Cynthia S., Bethany R., Rachel P. and Melissa S. | Bethany M., Amanda H., Jenna L. & April B. | Lisa S., Ashley G. & Amy S. | Diane B., Jill S., Nancy W., Mary W., Cindy R., Betty M., Merle D., Kathleen S. & Wendy W | Sara R., Brittany D., Erin R., Carly Z., Tiana M., Shannyn C., Ansonya B., Alana S., Marlene L., Deborah F., Rochelle S. & Carol B. | Renee D., Lisa C., Dacia P., Olivia V., Joelle S., Star G., Emily W. & Tracie G. | Ali M. & Jenny H. | Christien Roos of Penduka, Namibia

Heidi S. | Thank you, again, for making me sound more grammatically correct than I actually am. What a blessing you are!

And to the little lady who made me a momma; you've helped mold me into the woman I was called to be. I cannot wait to see what the Lord has up His sleeve for you, Alathea Grace. Your momma loves you so!

FIND OUT MORE ABOUT

penduka

SHOP THE PENDUKA STORE:
PENDUKALIFE.ORG/STORE

Have questions or a story to share?
We'd love to hear your thoughts about the book:
PENDUKALIFE.ORG/CONTACT

stay tuned for the
PENDUKA PODCAST | FALL 2016

CONNECT WITH JOY

facebook.com/simplybloom
Instagram.com/simplybloomjoy
joy@simplybloom.org

Invite Joy to speak at your next women's event:
SIMPLYBLOOM.ORG/SPEAKING

For more information about coaching & consulting:
SIMPLYBLOOM.ORG/COACHING

LIKE #HAPPYMAIL?

Write a note to Joy and she'll zip a quick note
of encouragement back to you:

Joy McMillan | PO Box 373 | Merrill, MI 48637

RECOMMENDED READING

- The Happiness Advantage *by* Shawn Achor
- Switch on Your Brain *by* Dr. Caroline Leaf
- Louder Than Words *by* Todd Henry
- Daring Greatly & Rising Strong *by* Brené Brown
- Scary Close *by* Donald Miller
- Boundaries *by* Cloud & Townsend
- Living Intentionally *by* John Maxwell
- The Compound Effect *by* Darren Hardy
- Big Magic *by* Elizabeth Gilbert
- Better Than Before *by* Gretchen Rubin
- Unglued & The Best Yes *by* Lysa Terkeurst
- Essentialism *by* Greg McKeown
- The One Thing *by* Gary Keller & Jay Papasan
- The Go-Giver *by* Bob Burg
- The Art of Neighboring *by* Jay Pathak
- The Art of Work *by* Jeff Goins
- The Shack *by* Paul W. Young

MY FAVORITE PODCASTS:

- The EntreLeadership Podcast
- Read to Lead *with* Jeff Brown
- This Is Your Life *with* Michael Hyatt
- The Life Coach School Podcast *with* Brooke Castillo
- Andy Stanley Leadership Podcast
- The Portfolio Life *with* Jeff Goins
- 48 Days *with* Dan Miller
- Happy Hour *with* Jamie Ivey
- The Influence Podcast
- Red Rocks Church
- iBethel (Kris Vallotton & Bill Johnson)
- Elevation Church

ABOUT THE AUTHOR

Joy McMillan is the founder of *Simply Bloom Productions LLC*, a creative little company with a big heart and an even bigger dream.

A writer, speaker, graphic designer, mentor & coach, she loves helping women embrace their stories, live out their purpose with passion, and leave legacies of love.

Founder of the #weROARproject and creative whirlwind behind the Simply Bloom shop, she's the author of *XES, The New Author's Launch Manual* & *Penduka*.

Originally hailing from Southern Africa, Joy lives and loves in Michigan with her hubby and their two little loin-fruit.

NOTES

CHAPTER 1:
[1] www.goodthinkinc.com
[2] ROAR : Random | Otherly | Affirmation | Revolution (you can find out more about the project, and download free printable cards, at weroarproject.org)

CHAPTER 2:
[3] Proverbs 23:7
[4] http://drleaf.com/media/page2/
[5] www.drleaf.com/about/toxic-thoughts/
[6] www.robertmadu.com

CHAPTER 3:
[7] www.jessconnolly.com

CHAPTER 4:
[8] www.lovingonpurpose.com

CHAPTER 5:
[9] www.simplybloom.org/2014/06/on-being-rooted-confessions-of-an-approval-addict-plus-free-printable.html
[10] This story is originally attributed to Zig Ziglar and has been retold many times over the years. Several versions can be found online.

CHAPTER 6:
[11] Genesis 3:8 "Then the man and his wife heard the sound of the Lord God as he was walking in the garden in the cool of the day, and they hid from the Lord God among the trees of the garden."

CHAPTER 7:
[12] www.puttylike.com/about

CHAPTER 8:
[13] "But he said to me, "My grace is sufficient for you, for my power is made perfect in weakness." Therefore I will boast all the more gladly about my weaknesses, so that Christ's power may rest on me."
[14] www.strengthsfinder.com/home.aspx
[15] www.saddlebackresources.com/collections/shape

CHAPTER 9:
[16] www.48days.com
[17] http://amzn.to/1QHxUGR

CHAPTER 12:
[18] I'm a member of this amazing network of creative women:
www.theinfluencenetwork.com
[19] The long, juicy version of my story can be found at the end of my book, XES

CHAPTER 15:
[20] www.ibtimes.co.uk/monaco-richest-place-earth-1454967
[21] http://amzn.to/1QPo5RI

CHAPTER 16:
[22] http://amzn.to/1Udb4q9
[23] http://amzn.to/1QPt7NF
[24] http://amzn.to/1LJy9tx

CHAPTER 17:
[25] "Do nothing out of selfish ambition or vain conceit. Rather, in humility value others above yourselves" Philippians 2:3

CHAPTER 19:
[26] http://amzn.to/1QrxRPo
[27] http://www.emilyley.com/

CHAPTER 20:
[28] IBM Operating System/360 Concepts and Facilities by Witt and Ward. IBM Systems Reference Library. File Number: S360-36
[29] www.psychologytoday.com/blog/rewired-the-psychology-technology/201407/our-social-media-obsession,
www.cnn.com/2011/HEALTH/07/28/ep.smartphone.obsessed.cohen/index.html
www.ragan.com/Main/Articles/90_percent_of_young_people_wake_up_with_their_smar_45989.aspx
[30] www.5lovelanguages.com
[31] by Greg McKeown: http://amzn.to/1Qrliwf
[32] by Gary Keller & Jay Papasan : http://amzn.to/1Qrllb8
[33] www.apa.org/research/action/multitask.aspx
[34] www.interruptions.net/literature/CubeSmart-productivity-wp1.pdf and
www.timharford.com/2015/09/multi-tasking-how-to-survive-in-the-21st-century/
[35] www.toddhenry.com/

CHAPTER 21:
[36] John 10:10

54628563R00147

Made in the USA
Charleston, SC
07 April 2016